Contents

THAI CUCUMBER SALAD	
BEST BROILED TOMATO SANDWICH	
BEET SALAD WITH GOAT CHEESE	7
CRANBERRY AND CILANTRO QUINOA SALAD	8
CUBAN MIDNIGHT SANDWICH	8
JERRE'S BLACK BEAN AND PORK TENDERLOIN SLOW COOKER CHILI	9
SAUSAGE, POTATO AND KALE SOUP	10
CURRIED BUTTERNUT SQUASH AND PEAR SOUP	10
CREAMY MUSHROOM SOUP	11
SLOW COOKER BBQ CHICKEN	12
UKRAINIAN RED BORSCHT SOUP	13
HEAVENLY EGG SALAD	13
GRILLED PEANUT BUTTER AND JELLY SANDWICH	14
ESPINACAS CON GARBANZOS (SPINACH WITH GARBANZO BEANS)	15
MARINATED CUCUMBER, ONION, AND TOMATO SALAD	15
LEMON CHICKEN ORZO SOUP	16
PARMESAN BRUSSELS SPROUTS	17
SALAD WITH BASIL MAYO DRESSING	17
SUMMER CORN SALAD	18
ITALIAN GRILLED CHEESE SANDWICHES	19
SIMPLE SWEET AND SPICY CHICKEN WRAPS	19
BEER BRATS	20
TURKEY CARCASS SOUP	21
GREEK PASTA SALAD	22
GREEN SALAD WITH CRANBERRY VINAIGRETTE	23
STEAK SOUP	23
CHICKEN, ASPARAGUS, AND MUSHROOM SKILLET	24
ROASTED CAULIFLOWER SOUP	25
HOT DOG CHILI	26
MANDARIN CHICKEN PASTA SALAD	27
GRILLED PEANUT BUTTER AND BANANA SANDWICH	27
PESTO GRILLED CHEESE SANDWICH	28

CHICKEN CLUB PASTA SALAD	29
BAKED MAC AND CHEESE FOR ONE	29
LEBANESE-STYLE RED LENTIL SOUP	30
CREAMY CUCUMBER SALAD	31
CHAKCHOUKA (SHAKSHOUKA)	31
SPICY SWEET POTATO AND COCONUT SOUP	32
SHRIMP AND GRITS	33
SIMPLE STROMBOLI	34
SUN-DRIED TOMATO BASIL ORZO	35
SPICED BUTTERNUT SQUASH SOUP	35
KRISTA'S STICKY HONEY GARLIC WINGS	36
DARRA'S FAMOUS TUNA WALDORF SALAD SANDWICH FILLING	37
CHEESY POTATO SALAD	38
THAI CURRY SOUP	38
SOUTHERN DILL POTATO SALAD	39
CREAM OF CARROT SOUP	40
SLOW COOKER SPICY CHICKEN	41
MEXICAN BEAN AND RICE SALAD	41
CLASSIC LASAGNA	42
BUFFALO CHICKEN WRAPS	43
SESAME NOODLE SALAD	43
TUNA MELTS	44
TOMATO BASIL SOUP	45
BEST BEAN SALAD	45
GOURMET CHICKEN SANDWICH	46
JAN'S PRETZEL DOGS	47
SOUTHERN FRIED CABBAGE WITH BACON, MUSHROOMS, AND ONIONS	48
TANGY TURKEY AND SWISS SANDWICHES	48
BLT WRAPS	49
BEEF CHIMICHANGAS	50
TURKEY WILD RICE SOUP	50
SPINACH BASIL PASTA SALAD	51
SPAGHETTI SQUASH WITH PINE NUTS, SAGE, AND ROMANO	52
CRESCENT DOGS	53

BREAD MACHINE PUMPERNICKEL BREAD	53
IRISH BACON AND CABBAGE SOUP	54
MEL'S CRAB SALAD	54
GRILLED PIZZA WRAPS	55
TOMATO GORGONZOLA SOUP	55
SPECIAL LOBSTER BISQUE	56
BUFFALO CHICKEN CHILI	57
CRAB LEGS WITH GARLIC BUTTER SAUCE	58
COCONUT CURRY PUMPKIN SOUP	58
ROASTED CARROT SALAD	59
TONYA'S TERRIFIC SLOPPY JOES	59
JALAPENO POPPER GRILLED CHEESE SANDWICH	60
ROASTED CAULIFLOWER AND LEEK SOUP	61
BEAN WITH BACON	62
POTATO SALAD	62
CAJUN SHRIMP	63
MANDI'S CHEESY POTATO SOUP	64
THAI SPICY BASIL CHICKEN FRIED RICE	64
CABBAGE AND SMOKED SAUSAGE PASTA	65
CARAMELIZED BUTTERNUT SQUASH SOUP	66
ROASTED TOMATO SOUP	66
CALIFORNIA MELT	67
QUICK AND SUPER EASY CHICKEN AND DUMPLINGS	68
VEGAN BLACK BEAN BURGERS	68
SHRIMP AND PASTA SHELL SALAD	69
HAM AND BEANS AND MORE	70
PESTO PASTA CAPRESE SALAD	71
CAPRESE SALAD WITH BALSAMIC REDUCTION	72
CLASSIC CUBAN MIDNIGHT (MEDIANOCHE) SANDWICH	72
EASY CLOUD BREAD	73
CREAMY TOMATO-BASIL SOUP	74
VIETNAMESE SANDWICH	74
STEF'S SUPER CHEESY GARLIC BREAD	75
HEARTY CHICKEN AND RICE SOUP	76

TORTELLINI, STEAK, AND CAESAR	76
HEARTY CHICKEN AND RICE SOUP	77
MIMI'S ZUCCHINI PIE	78
HALLOWEEN EYE OF NEWT	78
TURKEY SLOPPY JOES	79
VEGAN BROCCOLI SOUP	80
REUBEN SANDWICH	80
HAWAIIAN HAM AND CHEESE SLIDERS	81
SPINACH AND BACON QUICHE	82
TRADITIONAL CREAMY COLESLAW	82
CREAM OF ASPARAGUS AND MUSHROOM SOUP	83
HEARTY VEGAN SLOW-COOKER CHILI	84
QUINOA VEGETABLE SALAD	85
ITALIAN SUBS - RESTAURANT STYLE	86
JIM'S CHEDDAR ONION SODA BREAD	87
CHILI RELLENO CASSEROLE	87
BLT	88
SLOW COOKER GERMAN-STYLE PORK ROAST WITH SAUERKRAUT AND POTATOES	89
SPICY GRILLED CHEESE SANDWICH	89
SPENCE'S PESTO CHICKEN PASTA	90
HARVEY HAM SANDWICHES	91
SPICY GRILLED CHEESE SANDWICH	91
BEST GREEK QUINOA SALAD	92
MOTHER-IN-LAW EGGS	92
SHRIMP QUESADILLAS	93
EMERGENCY GARLIC BREAD	94
BLACK BEAN, CORN, AND TOMATO SALAD WITH FETA CHEESE	94
OPEN-FACED BROILED ROAST BEEF SANDWICH	95
HAM SALAD	96
SUPER SEVEN SPINACH SALAD	96
QUICK TUNA SALAD	97
GRILLED CORN SALAD	97
SOUTHERN YANK PULLED PORK BBQ	98
OYAKODON (JAPANESE CHICKEN AND EGG RICE BOWL)	98

MENDOCINO CHICKEN SALAD	99
DOUBLE DECKER TACOS	100
GREEK COUSCOUS	101
GREEK ZOODLE SALAD	101
MEATLOAF CUPCAKES	102

THAI CUCUMBER SALAD

Servings: 4 | Prep: 15m | Cooks: 30m | Total: 45m

NUTRITION FACTS

Calories: 238 | Carbohydrates: 37.1g | Fat: 9.4g | Protein: 5.8g | Cholesterol: 0mg

INGREDIENTS

- 3 large cucumbers, peeled, halved lengthwise, seeded, and cut into 1/4-inch slices
- 2 jalapeno peppers, seeded and chopped
- 1 tablespoon salt
- 1/4 cup chopped cilantro
- 1/2 cup white sugar
- 1/2 cup chopped peanuts
- 1/2 cup rice wine vinegar

DIRECTIONS

1. Toss the cucumbers with the salt in a colander, and leave in the sink to drain for 30 minutes. Rinse with cold water, then drain and pat dry with paper towels.
2. Whisk together the sugar and vinegar in a mixing bowl until the sugar has dissolved. Add the cucumbers, jalapeno peppers, and cilantro; toss to combine. Sprinkle chopped peanuts on top before serving.

BEST BROILED TOMATO SANDWICH

Servings: 2 | Prep: 10m | Cooks: 5m | Total: 15m

NUTRITION FACTS

Calories: 509 | Carbohydrates: 43.2g | Fat: 34.8g | Protein: 9.6g | Cholesterol: 14mg

INGREDIENTS

- 2 tablespoons olive oil
- 1/4 teaspoon dried oregano
- 2 tablespoons balsamic vinegar
- 1/4 teaspoon black pepper
- 4 ripe tomatoes, sliced
- 3 tablespoons grated Parmesan cheese, divided
- 3 tablespoons mayonnaise
- 4 slices bread, lightly toasted
- 1/2 teaspoon dried parsley

DIRECTIONS

1. Preheat oven to broil.
2. In a shallow bowl, whisk together the olive oil and vinegar. Marinate the tomatoes in the mixture, stirring occasionally.
3. Meanwhile, in a small bowl, combine mayonnaise, parsley, oregano, black pepper and 4 teaspoons Parmesan cheese. Spread mixture on each slice of toasted bread. Place marinated tomatoes on 2 slices and sprinkle with remaining Parmesan cheese.
4. Place on a baking sheet and broil for 5 minutes, or until cheese turns golden brown. Serve immediately, open faced or closed.

BEET SALAD WITH GOAT CHEESE
Servings: 6 | Prep: 10m | Cooks: 30m | Total: 40m

NUTRITION FACTS

Calories: 347 | Carbohydrates: 25g | Fat: 26.1g | Protein: 5.3g | Cholesterol: 7mg

INGREDIENTS

- 4 medium beets - scrubbed, trimmed and cut in half
- 1/2 cup frozen orange juice concentrate
- 1/3 cup chopped walnuts
- 1/4 cup balsamic vinegar
- 3 tablespoons maple syrup
- 1/2 cup extra-virgin olive oil
- 1 (10 ounce) package mixed baby salad greens
- 2 ounces goat cheese

DIRECTIONS

1. Place beets into a saucepan, and fill with enough water to cover. Bring to a boil, then cook for 20 to 30 minutes, until tender. Drain and cool, then cut in to cubes.
2. While the beets are cooking, place the walnuts in a skillet over medium-low heat. Heat until warm and starting to toast, then stir in the maple syrup. Cook and stir until evenly coated, then remove from the heat and set aside to cool.
3. In a small bowl, whisk together the orange juice concentrate, balsamic vinegar and olive oil to make the dressing.
4. Place a large helping of baby greens onto each of four salad plates, divide candied walnuts equally and sprinkle over the greens. Place equal amounts of beets over the greens, and top with dabs of goat cheese. Drizzle each plate with some of the dressing.

CRANBERRY AND CILANTRO QUINOA SALAD

Servings: 6 | Prep: 10m | Cooks: 20m | Total: 2h30m

NUTRITION FACTS

Calories: 176 | Carbohydrates: 31.6g | Fat: 3.9g | Protein: 5.4g | Cholesterol: 0mg

INGREDIENTS

- 1 1/2 cups water
- 1/4 cup chopped fresh cilantro
- 1 cup uncooked quinoa, rinsed
- 1 lime, juiced
- 1/4 cup red bell pepper, chopped
- 1/4 cup toasted sliced almonds
- 1/4 cup yellow bell pepper, chopped
- 1/2 cup minced carrots
- 1 small red onion, finely chopped
- 1/2 cup dried cranberries
- 1 1/2 teaspoons curry powder
- salt and ground black pepper to taste

DIRECTIONS

1. Pour the water into a saucepan, and cover with a lid. Bring to a boil over high heat, then pour in the quinoa, recover, and continue to simmer over low heat until the water has been absorbed, 15 to 20 minutes. Scrape into a mixing bowl, and chill in the refrigerator until cold.
2. Once cold, stir in the red bell pepper, yellow bell pepper, red onion, curry powder, cilantro, lime juice, sliced almonds, carrots, and cranberries. Season to taste with salt and pepper. Chill before serving.

CUBAN MIDNIGHT SANDWICH

Servings: 4 | Prep: 20m | Cooks: 5m | Total: 25m

NUTRITION FACTS

Calories: 1096 | Carbohydrates: 44.1g | Fat: 84.4g | Protein: 43.3g | Cholesterol: 127mg

INGREDIENTS

- 1 cup mayonnaise
- 1/2 pound thinly sliced cooked ham
- 5 tablespoons Italian dressing
- 1/2 cheese

- 4 hoagie rolls, split lengthwise
- 1 cup dill pickle slices
- 4 tablespoons prepared mustard
- 1/2 cup olive oil
- 1/2 pound thinly sliced deli turkey meat

DIRECTIONS

1. In a small bowl, mix together mayonnaise and Italian dressing. Spread mixture on hoagie rolls. Spread each roll with mustard. On each roll, arrange layers of turkey, ham, and cheese. Top each with dill pickle slices. Close sandwiches, and brush tops and bottoms with olive oil.
2. Heat a non-stick skillet over medium high heat. Place sandwiches in skillet. Cook sandwiches for 2 minutes, pressing down with a plate covered with aluminum foil. Flip, and cook for 2 more minutes, or until cheese is melted. Remove from heat, place on plates, and cut in half diagonally.

JERRE'S BLACK BEAN AND PORK TENDERLOIN SLOW COOKER CHILI

Servings: 8 | Prep: 10m | Cooks: 10m | Total: 10h10m

NUTRITION FACTS

Calories: 245 | Carbohydrates: 31.9g | Fat: 2.8g | Protein: 24g | Cholesterol: 37mg

INGREDIENTS

- 1 1/2 pounds pork tenderloin, cut into 2 inch strips
- 1/2 cup chicken broth
- 1 small onion, coarsely chopped
- 1 teaspoon dried oregano
- 1 small red bell pepper, coarsely chopped
- 1 teaspoon ground cumin
- 3 (15 ounce) cans black beans
- 2 teaspoons chili powder
- 1 (16 ounce) jar salsa

DIRECTIONS

3. Combine pork tenderloin, onion, red pepper, black beans, salsa, chicken broth, oregano, cumin, and chili powder in a slow cooker. Set to Low and cook for 8 to 10 hours.
4. Break up pieces of cooked pork to thicken the chili before serving.

SAUSAGE, POTATO AND KALE SOUP

Servings: 12 | Prep: 10m | Cooks: 50m | Total: 1hm

NUTRITION FACTS

Calories: 266 | Carbohydrates: 16.4g | Fat: 18g | Protein: 10.6g | Cholesterol: 49mg

INGREDIENTS

- 1 pound bulk Italian sausage
- 1 onion, chopped
- 4 cups half-and-half
- 1/2 teaspoon dried oregano
- 3 cups cubed potatoes
- 1/2 teaspoon red pepper flakes, or more to taste
- 2 cups low-sodium chicken broth
- 1/2 teaspoon ground black pepper
- 2 cups whole milk
- 2 cups torn kale leaves (bite-size pieces)

DIRECTIONS

1. Heat a large soup pot over medium-high heat. Crumble sausage into pot; cook and stir until browned, about 10 minutes. Drain and discard grease.
2. Stir half-and-half, potatoes, chicken broth, milk, onion, oregano, and red pepper flakes into sausage, bring to a boil, and reduce heat to low. Simmer until potatoes are tender, about 30 minutes. Season with black pepper; stir kale into soup. Simmer until kale is tender, 10 to 15 more minutes.

CURRIED BUTTERNUT SQUASH AND PEAR SOUP

Servings: 8 | Prep: 15m | Cooks: 1h30m | Total: 1h45m

NUTRITION FACTS

Calories: 169 | Carbohydrates: 27.6g | Fat: 6.7g | Protein: 3.1g | Cholesterol: 20mg

INGREDIENTS

- 1 (2 pound) butternut squash
- 1 tablespoon curry powder
- 3 tablespoons unsalted butter
- 1 teaspoon salt
- 1 onion, diced
- 4 cups reduced sodium chicken broth

- 2 cloves garlic, minced
- 2 firm ripe Bartlett pears, peeled, cored, and cut into 1 inch dice
- 2 teaspoons minced fresh ginger root
- 1/2 cup half and half

DIRECTIONS

1. Preheat an oven to 375 degrees F (190 degrees C). Line a rimmed baking sheet with parchment paper.
2. Cut squash in half lengthwise; discard seeds and membrane. Place squash halves, cut sides down, on the prepared baking sheet. Roast in preheated oven until very soft, about 45 minutes. Scoop the pulp from the peel, and reserve.
3. Melt butter in a large soup pot over medium heat. Stir in the onion, garlic, ginger, curry powder, and salt. Cook and stir until the onion is soft, about 10 minutes. Pour the chicken broth into the pot, and bring to a boil. Stir in the pears and the reserved squash, and simmer until the pears are very soft, about 30 minutes.
4. Pour the soup into a blender, filling the pitcher no more than halfway full. Hold down the lid of the blender with a folded kitchen towel, and carefully start the blender. Puree in batches until smooth. Return the soup to the pot, stir in the half and half, and reheat.

CREAMY MUSHROOM SOUP

Servings: 6 | Prep: 15m | Cooks: 1h20m | Total: 1h35m

NUTRITION FACTS

Calories: 272 | Carbohydrates: 12.2g | Fat: 23.3g | Protein: 6.9g | Cholesterol: 78mg

INGREDIENTS

- 1/4 cup unsalted butter
- 2 cloves garlic, peeled
- 2 pounds sliced fresh mushrooms
- 4 cups chicken broth
- 1 pinch salt
- 1 cup water
- 1 yellow onion, diced
- 1 cup heavy whipping cream
- 1 1/2 tablespoons all-purpose flour
- 1 pinch salt and freshly ground black pepper to taste
- 6 sprigs fresh thyme
- 1 teaspoon fresh thyme leaves for garnish, or to taste

DIRECTIONS

1. Melt butter in a large soup pot over medium-high heat; cook mushrooms in butter with 1 pinch salt until the mushrooms give off their juices; reduce heat to low. Continue to cook, stirring often, until juices evaporate and the mushrooms are golden brown, about 15 minutes. Set aside a few attractive mushroom slices for garnish later, if desired. Mix onion into mushrooms and cook until onion is soft and translucent, about 5 more minutes.
2. Stir flour into mushroom mixture and cook, stirring often, for 2 minutes to remove raw flour taste. Tie thyme sprigs into a small bundle with kitchen twine and add to mushroom mixture; add garlic cloves. Pour chicken stock and water into mushroom mixture. Bring to a simmer and cook for 1 hour. Remove thyme bundle.
3. Transfer soup to a blender in small batches and puree on high speed until smooth and thick.
4. Return soup to pot and stir in cream. Season with salt and black pepper and serve in bowls, garnished with reserved mushroom slices and a few thyme leaves.

SLOW COOKER BBQ CHICKEN

Servings: 8 | Prep: 5m | Cooks: 6h30m | Total: 6h35m

NUTRITION FACTS

Calories: 589 | Carbohydrates: 90g | Fat: 9.5g | Protein: 34.2g | Cholesterol: 59mg

INGREDIENTS

- 4 large skinless, boneless chicken breast halves
- 2 tablespoons Worcestershire sauce
- 1 cup ketchup
- 1/2 teaspoon chili powder
- 2 tablespoons mustard
- 1/8 teaspoon cayenne pepper
- 2 teaspoons lemon juice
- 2 dashes hot pepper sauce, or to taste (optional)
- 1/4 teaspoon garlic powder
- 8 sandwich rolls, split
- 1/2 cup maple syrup

DIRECTIONS

1. Place the chicken breasts into the bottom of a slow cooker. In a bowl, stir together the ketchup, mustard, lemon juice, garlic powder, maple syrup, Worcestershire sauce, chili powder, cayenne pepper, and hot sauce until the mixture is well blended.
2. Pour the sauce over the chicken, set the cooker to Low, and cook for 6 hours. Shred the chicken with two forks, and cook for 30 more minutes. Serve the chicken and sauce spooned into the sandwich rolls.

UKRAINIAN RED BORSCHT SOUP

Servings: 10 | Prep: 25m | Cooks: 40m | Total: 1h5m

NUTRITION FACTS

Calories: 257 | Carbohydrates: 24.4g | Fat: 13.8g | Protein: 10.1g | Cholesterol: 31mg

INGREDIENTS

- 1 (16 ounce) package pork sausage
- 1/2 medium head cabbage, cored and shredded
- 3 medium beets, peeled and shredded
- 1 (8 ounce) can diced tomatoes, drained
- 3 carrots, peeled and shredded
- 3 cloves garlic, minced
- 3 medium baking potatoes, peeled and cubed
- salt and pepper to taste
- 1 tablespoon vegetable oil
- 1 teaspoon white sugar, or to taste
- 1 medium onion, chopped
- 1/2 cup sour cream, for topping
- 1 (6 ounce) can tomato paste
- 1 tablespoon chopped fresh parsley for garnish
- 3/4 cup water

DIRECTIONS

1. Crumble the sausage (if using) into a skillet over medium-high heat. Cook and stir until no longer pink. Remove from the heat and set aside.
2. Fill a large pot halfway with water(about 2 quarts), and bring to a boil. Add the sausage, and cover the pot. Return to a boil. Add the beets, and cook until they have lost their color. Add the carrots and potatoes, and cook until tender, about 15 minutes. Add the cabbage, and the can of diced tomatoes.
3. Heat the oil in a skillet over medium heat. Add the onion, and cook until tender. Stir in the tomato paste and water until well blended. Transfer to the pot. Add the raw garlic to the soup, cover and turn off the heat. Let stand for 5 minutes. Taste, and season with salt, pepper and sugar.
4. Ladle into serving bowls, and garnish with sour cream, if desired, and fresh parsley.

HEAVENLY EGG SALAD

Servings: 4 | Prep: 5m | Cooks: 16m | Total: 21m

NUTRITION FACTS

Calories: 212 | Carbohydrates: 3.2g | Fat: 18.4g | Protein: 9.9g | Cholesterol: 284mg

INGREDIENTS

- 6 eggs
- 1/2 lemon, juiced
- 1/4 cup mayonnaise
- 1/4 cup chopped green onions
- 1 teaspoon Dijon mustard
- salt and pepper to taste
- 1/2 teaspoon prepared yellow mustard

DIRECTIONS

1. Place egg in a saucepan and cover with cold water. Bring water to a boil and immediately remove from heat. Cover and let eggs stand in hot water for 10 to 12 minutes. Remove from hot water, cool and peel. For faster cooling, place the eggs in an ice bath before peeling.
2. In a medium bowl, stir together the mayonnaise, Dijon mustard, yellow mustard, lemon juice and green onions. Chop the eggs into big chunks and mix gently with the dressing. Season with salt and pepper.

GRILLED PEANUT BUTTER AND JELLY SANDWICH

Servings: 1 | Prep: 5m | Cooks: 8m | Total: 13m

NUTRITION FACTS

Calories: 273 | Carbohydrates: 35.5g | Fat: 12.5g | Protein: 5.3g | Cholesterol: 22mg

INGREDIENTS

- 2 teaspoons butter
- 1 teaspoon peanut butter
- 2 slices white bread
- 2 teaspoons any flavor fruit jelly

DIRECTIONS

1. Heat griddle or skillet to 350 degrees F (175 degrees C).
2. Spread butter on one side of each slice of bread. Spread peanut butter on unbuttered side of one slice of bread, and jelly on the other. Place one slice, buttered side down on the griddle. Top with other slice, so that peanut butter and jelly are in the middle. Cook for 4 minutes on each side, or until golden brown, and heated through.

ESPINACAS CON GARBANZOS (SPINACH WITH GARBANZO BEANS)

Servings: 4 | Prep: 15m | Cooks: 10m | Total: 25m

NUTRITION FACTS

Calories: 169 | Carbohydrates: 26g | Fat: 4.9g | Protein: 7.3g | Cholesterol: 0mg

INGREDIENTS

- 1 tablespoon extra-virgin olive oil
- 1 (12 ounce) can garbanzo beans, drained
- 4 cloves garlic, minced
- 1/2 teaspoon cumin
- 1/2 onion, diced
- 1/2 teaspoon salt
- 1 (10 ounce) box frozen chopped spinach, thawed and drained well

DIRECTIONS

1. Heat the olive oil in a skillet over medium-low heat. Cook the garlic and onion in the oil until translucent, about 5 minutes. Stir in the spinach, garbanzo beans, cumin, and salt. Use your stirring spoon to lightly mash the beans as the mixture cooks. Allow to cook until thoroughly heated.

MARINATED CUCUMBER, ONION, AND TOMATO SALAD

Servings: 6 | Prep: 15m | Cooks: 2h | Total: 2h15m

NUTRITION FACTS

Calories: 156 | Carbohydrates: 19.6g | Fat: 9.5g | Protein: 1.8g | Cholesterol: 0mg

INGREDIENTS

- 1 cup water
- 1 tablespoon fresh, coarsely ground black pepper
- 1/2 cup distilled white vinegar
- 3 cucumbers, peeled and sliced 1/4-inch thick
- 1/4 cup vegetable oil
- 3 tomatoes, cut into wedges
- 1/4 cup sugar
- 1 onion, sliced and separated into rings
- 2 teaspoons salt

DIRECTIONS

1. Whisk water, vinegar, oil, sugar, salt, and pepper together in a large bowl until smooth; add cucumbers, tomatoes, and onion and stir to coat.
2. Cover bowl with plastic wrap; refrigerate at least 2 hours.

LEMON CHICKEN ORZO SOUP
Servings: 12 | Prep: 20m | Cooks: 1h | Total: 1h20m

NUTRITION FACTS

Calories: 167 | Carbohydrates: 21.7g | Fat: 4.1g | Protein: 12.1g | Cholesterol: 20mg

INGREDIENTS

- 8 ounces orzo pasta
- 1 bay leaf
- 1 teaspoon olive oil
- 3 (32 ounce) cartons fat-free, low-sodium chicken broth
- 3 carrots, chopped, or more to taste
- 1/2 cup fresh lemon juice
- 3 ribs celery, chopped
- 1 lemon, zested
- 1 onion, chopped
- 8 ounces cooked chicken breast, chopped
- 2 cloves garlic, minced
- 1 (8 ounce) package baby spinach leaves
- 1/2 teaspoon dried thyme
- 1 lemon, sliced for garnish (optional)
- 1/2 teaspoon dried oregano
- 1/4 cup grated Parmesan cheese (optional)
- salt and ground black pepper to taste

DIRECTIONS

1. Bring a large pot of lightly salted water to a boil. Cook orzo in the boiling water until partially cooked through but not yet soft, about 5 minutes; drain and rinse with cold water until cooled completely.
2. Heat olive oil in a large pot over medium heat. Cook and stir carrots, celery, and onion in hot oil until the vegetables begin to soften and the onion becomes translucent, 5 to 7 minutes. Add garlic; cook and stir until fragrant, about 1 minute more. Season mixture with thyme, oregano, salt, black pepper, and bay leaf; continue cooking another 30 seconds before pouring chicken broth into the pot

3. Bring the broth to a boil. Partially cover the pot, reduce heat to medium-low, and simmer until the vegetables are just tender, about 10 minutes.
4. Stir orzo, lemon juice, and lemon zest into the broth; add chicken. Cook until the chicken and orzo are heated through, about 5 minutes. Add baby spinach; cook until the spinach wilts into the broth and the orzo is tender, 2 to 3 minutes. Ladle soup into bowls; garnish with lemon slices and Parmesan cheese.

PARMESAN BRUSSELS SPROUTS

Servings: 2 | Prep: 10m | Cooks: 15m | Total: 25m

NUTRITION FACTS

Calories: 203 | Carbohydrates: 6.3g | Fat: 18.9g | Protein: 4.2g | Cholesterol: 50mg

INGREDIENTS

- 1 tablespoon butter
- 1 tablespoon butter
- 2 cloves garlic, chopped
- 2 tablespoons shredded Parmesan cheese, or more to taste
- 1 tablespoon butter
- salt and ground black pepper to taste
- 6 Brussels sprouts, trimmed and halved

DIRECTIONS

1. Heat a frying pan over medium heat until hot, 3 minutes. Melt 1 tablespoon butter; cook and stir garlic until fragrant, 30 seconds. Add 1 tablespoon butter and Brussels sprouts, cut-side down; cover and cook until golden brown, 4 to 6 minutes.
2. Flip Brussels sprouts; add 1 tablespoon butter. Cover and cook until other side is browned, about 3 more minutes. Transfer to a serving plate. Sprinkle with Parmesan cheese, salt, and black pepper.

SALAD WITH BASIL MAYO DRESSING

Servings: 4 | Prep: 15m | Cooks: 10m | Total: 25m

NUTRITION FACTS

Calories: 440 | Carbohydrates: 23.4g | Fat: 34.1g | Protein: 12.2g | Cholesterol: 31mg

INGREDIENTS

- 1/2 pound bacon

- 1 teaspoon salt
- 1/2 cup mayonnaise
- 1 teaspoon ground black pepper
- 2 tablespoons red wine vinegar
- 1 tablespoon canola oil
- 1/4 cup finely chopped fresh basil
- 1 pound romaine lettuce - rinsed, dried, and torn into bite-size pieces
- 4 slices French bread, cut into 1/2 inch pieces
- 1 pint cherry tomatoes, quartered

DIRECTIONS

1. Place bacon in a large, deep skillet. Cook over medium high heat until evenly brown. Drain, crumble and set aside, reserving 2 tablespoons of the drippings.
2. In a small bowl, whisk together the reserved bacon drippings, mayonnaise, vinegar and basil and let dressing stand, covered, at room temperature.
3. In a large skillet over medium heat, toss the bread pieces with the salt and pepper. Drizzle with the oil, continue tossing and cook over medium-low heat until golden brown.
4. In a large bowl mix together the romaine, tomatoes, bacon and croutons. Pour the dressing over the salad and toss well.

SUMMER CORN SALAD
Servings: 4 | Prep: 25m | Cooks: 20m | Total: 45m

NUTRITION FACTS

Calories: 305 | Carbohydrates: 42.8g | Fat: 15.6g | Protein: 6.2g | Cholesterol: 0mg

INGREDIENTS

- 6 ears corn, husked and cleaned
- 1/4 cup olive oil
- 3 large tomatoes, diced
- 2 tablespoons white vinegar
- 1 large onion, diced
- salt and pepper to taste
- 1/4 cup chopped fresh basil

DIRECTIONS

1. Bring a large pot of lightly salted water to a boil. Cook corn in boiling water for 7 to 10 minutes, or until desired tenderness. Drain, cool, and cut kernels off the cob with a sharp knife.

2. In a large bowl, toss together the corn, tomatoes, onion, basil, oil, vinegar, salt and pepper. Chill until serving.

ITALIAN GRILLED CHEESE SANDWICHES

Servings: 6 | Prep: 8m | Cooks: 7m | Total: 15m

NUTRITION FACTS

Calories: 394 | Carbohydrates: 42g | Fat: 18.3g | Protein: 15g | Cholesterol: 46mg

INGREDIENTS

- 1/4 cup unsalted butter
- 1 teaspoon dried oregano
- 1/8 teaspoon garlic powder (optional)
- 1 (8 ounce) package shredded mozzarella cheese
- 12 slices white bread
- 1 (24 ounce) jar vodka marinara sauce

DIRECTIONS

1. Preheat your oven's broiler.
2. Place 6 slices of bread onto a baking sheet. Spread a small handful of the mozzarella cheese over each slice. Top with the remaining 6 slices of bread. Mix together the butter and garlic powder, brush some over the tops of the sandwiches, or spread with the back of a tablespoon. Sprinkle with dried oregano.
3. Place baking sheet under the broiler for 2 to 3 minutes, until golden brown. Remove pan from oven, flip sandwiches, and brush the other sides with butter, and sprinkle with oregano. Return to the broiler, and cook until golden, about 2 minutes.
4. Cut sandwiches in half diagonally, and serve immediately with vodka sauce on the side for dipping.

SIMPLE SWEET AND SPICY CHICKEN WRAPS

Servings: 8 | Prep: 20m | Cooks: 15m | Total: 35m

NUTRITION FACTS

Calories: 488 | Carbohydrates: 44.7g | Fat: 22.6g | Protein: 26.6g | Cholesterol: 57mg

INGREDIENTS

- 1/2 cup mayonnaise
- 1 1/2 pounds skinless, boneless chicken breast halves - cut into thin strips
- 1/4 cup finely chopped seedless cucumber

- 1 cup thick and chunky salsa
- 1 tablespoon honey
- 1 tablespoon honey
- 1/2 teaspoon cayenne pepper
- 1/2 teaspoon cayenne pepper
- ground black pepper to taste
- 8 (10 inch) flour tortillas
- 2 tablespoons olive oil
- 1 (10 ounce) bag baby spinach leaves

DIRECTIONS

1. Mix together the mayonnaise, cucumber, 1 tablespoon of honey, 1/2 teaspoon of cayenne pepper, and black pepper in a bowl until smooth. Cover and refrigerate until needed.
2. Heat the olive oil in a skillet on medium-high heat, and cook and stir the chicken breast strips until they are beginning to turn golden and are no longer pink in the middle, about 8 minutes. Stir in the salsa, 1 tablespoon of honey, and 1/2 teaspoon of cayenne pepper. Reduce the heat to medium-low and simmer, stirring occasionally, until the flavors have blended, about 5 minutes.
3. Stack the tortillas, 4 at a time, in a microwave oven and heat until warm and pliable, 20 to 30 seconds per batch.
4. Spread each tortilla with 1 tablespoon of the mayonnaise-cucumber mixture, top with a layer of baby spinach leaves, and arrange about 1/2 cup of chicken mixture on the spinach leaves.
5. Fold the bottom of each tortilla up about 2 inches, and start rolling the burrito from the right side. When the burrito is half-rolled, fold the top of the tortilla down, enclosing the filling, and continue rolling to make a tight, compact cylinder.

BEER BRATS

Servings: 10 | Prep: 5m | Cooks: 20m | Total: 25m

NUTRITION FACTS

Calories: 382 | Carbohydrates: 9.7g | Fat: 27.4g | Protein: 13.8g | Cholesterol: 69mg

INGREDIENTS

- 4 (12 ounce) cans beer
- 1 teaspoon garlic powder
- 1 large onion, diced
- 1 teaspoon salt
- 10 bratwurst
- 1/2 teaspoon ground black pepper

- 2 teaspoons red pepper flakes

DIRECTIONS

1. Preheat an outdoor grill for medium-high heat. When hot, lightly oil grate.
2. Combine the beer and onions in a large pot; bring to a boil. Submerge the bratwurst in the beer; add the red pepper flakes, garlic powder, salt, and pepper. Reduce heat to medium and cook another 10 to 12 minutes. Remove the bratwurst from the beer mixture; reduce heat to low, and continue cooking the onions.
3. Cook the bratwurst on the preheated grill, turning once, 5 to 10 minutes. Serve with the beer mixture as a topping or side.

TURKEY CARCASS SOUP

Servings: 12 | Prep: 45m | Cooks: 2h | Total: 2h45m

NUTRITION FACTS

Calories: 133 | Carbohydrates: 27.7g | Fat: 1.3g | Protein: 4.2g | Cholesterol: 2mg

INGREDIENTS

- 1 turkey carcass
- 1 tablespoon Worcestershire sauce
- 4 quarts water
- 1 1/2 teaspoons salt
- 6 small potatoes, diced
- 1 teaspoon dried parsley
- 4 large carrots, diced
- 1 teaspoon dried basil
- 2 stalks celery, diced
- 1 bay leaf
- 1 large onion, diced
- 1/4 teaspoon freshly cracked black pepper
- 1 1/2 cups shredded cabbage
- 1/4 teaspoon paprika
- 1 (28 ounce) can whole peeled tomatoes, chopped
- 1/4 teaspoon poultry seasoning
- 1/2 cup uncooked barley
- 1 pinch dried thyme

DIRECTIONS

1. Place the turkey carcass into a large soup pot or stock pot and pour in the water; bring to a boil, reduce heat to a simmer, and cook the turkey frame until the remaining meat falls off the bones, about 1 hour. Remove the turkey carcass and remove and chop any remaining turkey meat. Chop the meat.
2. Strain the broth through a fine mesh strainer into a clean soup pot. Add the chopped turkey to the strained broth; bring the to a boil, reduce heat, and stir in the potatoes, carrots, celery, onion, cabbage, tomatoes, barley, Worcestershire sauce, salt, parsley, basil, bay leaf, black pepper, paprika, poultry seasoning, and thyme. Simmer until the vegetables are tender, about 1 more hour. Remove bay leaf before serving.

GREEK PASTA SALAD

Servings: 8 | Prep: 20m | Cooks: 10m | Total: 3h30m

NUTRITION FACTS

Calories: 307 | Carbohydrates: 19.3g | Fat: 23.6g | Protein: 5.4g | Cholesterol: 14mg

INGREDIENTS

- 2 cups penne pasta
- 10 cherry tomatoes, halved
- 1/4 cup red wine vinegar
- 1 small red onion, chopped
- 1 tablespoon lemon juice
- 1 green bell pepper, chopped
- 2 cloves garlic, crushed
- 1 red bell pepper, chopped
- 2 teaspoons dried oregano
- 1/2 cucumber, sliced
- salt and pepper to taste
- 1/2 cup sliced black olives
- 2/3 cup extra-virgin olive oil
- 1/2 cup crumbled feta cheese

DIRECTIONS

1. Fill a large pot with lightly salted water and bring to a rolling boil over high heat. Once the water is boiling, stir in the penne, and return to a boil. Cook the pasta uncovered, stirring occasionally, until the pasta has cooked through, but is still firm to the bite, about 11 minutes. Rinse with cold water and drain well in a colander set in the sink.
2. Whisk together the vinegar, lemon juice, garlic, oregano, salt, pepper, and olive oil. Set aside.

    Combine pasta, tomatoes, onion, green and red peppers, cucumber, olives, and feta cheese in a large bowl. Pour vinaigrette over the pasta and mix together. Cover and chill for 3 hours before serving.

GREEN SALAD WITH CRANBERRY VINAIGRETTE

Servings: 8 | Prep: 15m | Cooks: 5m | Total: 20m

NUTRITION FACTS

Calories: 218 | Carbohydrates: 6.2g | Fat: 19.2g | Protein: 6.5g | Cholesterol: 11mg

INGREDIENTS

- 1 cup sliced almonds
- 1/2 teaspoon salt
- 3 tablespoons red wine vinegar
- 1/2 teaspoon ground black pepper
- 1/3 cup olive oil
- 2 tablespoons water
- 1/4 cup fresh cranberries
- 1/2 red onion, thinly sliced
- 1 tablespoon Dijon mustard
- 4 ounces crumbled blue cheese
- 1/2 teaspoon minced garlic
- 1 pound mixed salad greens

DIRECTIONS

1. Preheat oven to 375 degrees F (190 degrees C). Arrange almonds in a single layer on a baking sheet. Toast in oven for 5 minutes, or until nuts begin to brown.
2. In a blender or food processor, combine the vinegar, oil, cranberries, mustard, garlic, salt, pepper, and water. Process until smooth.
3. In a large bowl, toss the almonds, onion, blue cheese, and greens with the vinegar mixture until evenly coated.

STEAK SOUP

Servings: 8 | Prep: 45m | Cooks: 1h30m | Total: 2h15m

NUTRITION FACTS

Calories: 361 | Carbohydrates: 26.9g | Fat: 12.9g | Protein: 36g | Cholesterol: 84mg

INGREDIENTS

- 2 tablespoons butter
- 4 sprigs fresh parsley, chopped
- 2 tablespoons vegetable oil

- 2 tablespoons chopped celery leaves
- 1 1/2 pounds lean boneless beef round steak, cut into cubes
- 1 bay leaf
- 1/2 cup chopped onion
- 1/2 teaspoon dried marjoram
- 3 tablespoons all-purpose flour
- 1 1/2 cups peeled, diced Yukon Gold potatoes
- 1 tablespoon paprika
- 1 ½ cups sliced carrots
- 1 teaspoon salt
- 1 1/2 cups chopped celery
- 1/4 teaspoon ground black pepper
- 1 (6 ounce) can tomato paste
- 4 cups beef broth
- 1 (15.25 ounce) can whole kernel corn, drained
- 2 cups water

DIRECTIONS

1. Melt butter and oil in a large skillet over medium heat until the foam disappears from the butter, and stir in the steak cubes and onion. Cook and stir until the meat and onion are browned, about 10 minutes. While beef is cooking, mix together flour, paprika, salt, and pepper in a bowl. Sprinkle the flour mixture over the browned meat, and stir to coat.
2. In a large soup pot, pour in the beef broth and water, and stir in the parsley, celery leaves, bay leaf, and marjoram. Stir in beef mixture, and bring to a boil. Reduce heat to medium-low, cover the pot, and simmer, stirring occasionally, until meat is tender, about 45 minutes.
3. Mix in the potatoes, carrots, celery, tomato paste, and corn; bring the soup back to a simmer, and cook uncovered, stirring occasionally, until the vegetables are tender and the soup is thick, 15 to 20 minutes. Remove bay leaf and serve hot.

CHICKEN, ASPARAGUS, AND MUSHROOM SKILLET
Servings: 2 | Prep: 15m | Cooks: 25m | Total: 40m

NUTRITION FACTS

Calories: 430 | Carbohydrates: 7.3g | Fat: 33.5g | Protein: 26.9g | Cholesterol: 107mg

INGREDIENTS

- 3 tablespoons butter
- 1/4 teaspoon salt

- 2 tablespoons olive oil
- 1 1/2 teaspoons lemon juice
- 1/2 teaspoon dried parsley
- 1 1/2 teaspoons white cooking wine
- 1/2 teaspoon dried basil
- 2 skinless, boneless chicken breast halves, sliced
- 1/8 teaspoon dried oregano
- 1/2 pound fresh asparagus, trimmed and cut into thirds
- 1 1/2 cloves garlic, minced
- 1 cup sliced fresh mushrooms

DIRECTIONS

1. Melt the butter with the olive oil in a skillet over medium-high; stir the parsley, basil, oregano, garlic, salt, lemon juice, and wine into the butter mixture. Add the chicken; cook and stir until the chicken is browned, about 3 minutes. Reduce heat to medium; cook, stirring occasionally, until the chicken is no longer pink inside, about 10 more minutes.
2. Add the asparagus; cook and stir until the asparagus is bright green and just starting to become tender, about 3 minutes. Stir in the mushrooms and cook an additional 3 minutes to let the mushrooms release their juice. Serve hot.

ROASTED CAULIFLOWER SOUP

Servings: 6 | Prep: 10m | Cooks: 1h | Total: 1h10m

NUTRITION FACTS

Calories: 135 | Carbohydrates: 13.2g | Fat: 7.6g | Protein: 4.4g | Cholesterol: 10mg

INGREDIENTS

- 1 head cauliflower, cut into small florets
- 1 tablespoon butter
- 2 tablespoons roasted garlic-flavored extra-virgin olive oil
- 1 onion, finely chopped
- 1/4 teaspoon ground nutmeg
- 3 tablespoons all-purpose flour
- 2 teaspoons garlic powder
- 1 (14 ounce) can chicken broth
- 1 1/2 teaspoons salt
- 1 cup milk
- 1/2 teaspoon ground black pepper
- 1 tablespoon dry sherry

DIRECTIONS

1. Preheat oven to 450 degrees F (230 degrees C).
2. Place the cauliflower in a small roasting pan. Drizzle with oil and season with nutmeg, garlic powder, salt, and pepper; toss to coat.
3. Roast the cauliflower in the preheated oven stirring every 10 minutes until golden brown and tender, 30 to 40 minutes. Remove from the oven and set aside.
4. Melt the butter in a large saucepan over medium heat. Add the chopped onion and cook and stir until lightly golden brown, about 10 minutes.
5. Sprinkle the flour over the onions and stir to coat. Slowly pour the chicken broth and milk into the pan. Mix with a wire whisk until all of the flour is dissolved. Bring to a boil while stirring continuously until it thickens, then reduce heat to low. Stir in the sherry and the roasted cauliflower. Serve as is, or blend half and recombine with the rest of the soup for a thicker consistency.

HOT DOG CHILI

Servings: 6 | Prep: 10m | Cooks: 20m | Total: 30m

NUTRITION FACTS

Calories: 168 | Carbohydrates: 7.5g | Fat: 9.4g | Protein: 13.6g | Cholesterol: 47mg

INGREDIENTS

- 1 pound ground beef
- 1/2 teaspoon salt
- 1/3 cup water
- 1/2 teaspoon ground black pepper
- 1/2 (10 ounce) can tomato sauce
- 1/2 teaspoon white sugar
- 1/2 cup ketchup
- 1/2 teaspoon onion powder
- 2 1/2 teaspoons chili powder
- 1 dash Worcestershire sauce

DIRECTIONS

1. Place ground beef in a large saucepan with water and mash the beef with a potato masher to break apart. Stir in tomato sauce, ketchup, chili powder, salt, black pepper, sugar, onion powder, and Worcestershire sauce. Bring to a boil and cook over medium heat until the chili has thickened slightly and the beef is fully cooked, about 20 minutes.

MANDARIN CHICKEN PASTA SALAD

Servings: 6 | Prep: 45m | Cooks: 8m | Total: 53m

NUTRITION FACTS

Calories: 425 | Carbohydrates: 44.7g | Fat: 18.9g | Protein: 21.8g | Cholesterol: 35mg

INGREDIENTS

- 1 teaspoon finely chopped, peeled fresh ginger
- 1/2 cucumber - scored, halved lengthwise, seeded, and sliced
- 1/3 cup rice vinegar
- 1/2 cup diced red bell pepper
- 1/3 cup orange juice
- 1/2 cup coarsely chopped red onion
- 1/4 cup vegetable oil
- 2 diced Roma tomatoes
- 1 teaspoon toasted sesame oil
- 1 carrot, shredded
- 1 (1 ounce) package dry onion soup mix
- 1 (6 ounce) bag fresh spinach
- 2 teaspoons white sugar
- 1 (11 ounce) can mandarin orange segments, drained
- 1 clove garlic, pressed
- 2 cups diced cooked chicken
- 1 (8 ounce) package bow tie (farfalle) pasta
- 1/2 cup sliced almonds, toasted

DIRECTIONS

1. To make the dressing, whisk together the ginger root, rice vinegar, orange juice, vegetable oil, sesame oil, soup mix, sugar, and garlic until well blended. Cover, and refrigerate until needed.
2. Bring a large pot of lightly salted water to a boil. Add the bowtie pasta and cook for 8 to 10 minutes or until al dente; drain, and rinse under cold water. Place pasta in a large bowl.
3. To make the salad, toss the cucumber, bell pepper, onion, tomatoes, carrot, spinach, mandarin oranges, chicken, and almonds with the pasta. Pour the dressing over the salad mixture, and toss again to coat evenly. Serve immediately.

GRILLED PEANUT BUTTER AND BANANA SANDWICH

Servings: 1 | Prep: 2m | Cooks: 10m | Total: 12m

NUTRITION FACTS

Calories: 437 | Carbohydrates: 56.8g | Fat: 18.7g | Protein: 16.8g | Cholesterol: 0mg

INGREDIENTS

- cooking spray
- 2 slices whole wheat bread
- 2 tablespoons peanut butter
- 1 banana, sliced

DIRECTIONS

1. Heat a skillet or griddle over medium heat, and coat with cooking spray. Spread 1 tablespoon of peanut butter onto one side of each slice of bread. Place banana slices onto the peanut buttered side of one slice, top with the other slice and press together firmly. Fry the sandwich until golden brown on each side, about 2 minutes per side.

PESTO GRILLED CHEESE SANDWICH

Servings: 1 | Prep: 5m | Cooks: 10m | Total: 15m

NUTRITION FACTS

Calories: 503 | Carbohydrates: 24.2g | Fat: 36.5g | Protein: 20.4g | Cholesterol: 82mg

INGREDIENTS

- 2 slices Italian bread
- 1 slice provolone cheese
- 1 tablespoon softened butter, divided
- 2 slices tomato
- 1 tablespoon prepared pesto sauce, divided
- 1 slice American cheese

DIRECTIONS

1. Spread one side of a slice of bread with butter, and place it, buttered side down, into a nonstick skillet over medium heat.
2. Spread the top of the bread slice in the skillet with half the pesto sauce, and place a slice of provolone cheese, the tomato slices, and the slice of American cheese onto the pesto.
3. Spread remaining pesto sauce on one side of the second slice of bread, and place the bread slice, pesto side down, onto the sandwich. Butter the top side of the sandwich.
4. Gently fry the sandwich, flipping once, until both sides of the bread are golden brown and the cheese has melted, about 5 minutes per side.

CHICKEN CLUB PASTA SALAD

Servings: 6 | Prep: 20m | Cooks: 10m | Total: 30m

NUTRITION FACTS

Calories: 485 | Carbohydrates: 37.1g | Fat: 30.1g | Protein: 19.2g | Cholesterol: 48mg

INGREDIENTS

- 8 ounces corkscrew-shaped pasta
- 1 cup cubed Muenster cheese
- 3/4 cup Italian-style salad dressing
- 1 cup chopped celery
- 1/4 cup mayonnaise
- 1 cup chopped green bell pepper
- 2 cups chopped, cooked rotisserie chicken
- 8 ounces cherry tomatoes, halved
- 12 slices crispy cooked bacon, crumbled
- 1 avocado - peeled, pitted, and chopped

DIRECTIONS

1. Bring a large pot of lightly salted water to a boil. Cook pasta in the boiling water, stirring occasionally until cooked through but firm to the bite, 10 to 12 minutes. Drain and rinse under cold water.
2. Whisk Italian-style dressing and mayonnaise together in a large bowl. Stir pasta, chicken, bacon, Muenster cheese, celery, green bell pepper, cherry tomatoes, and avocado into dressing until evenly coated.

BAKED MAC AND CHEESE FOR ONE

Servings: 1 | Prep: 10m | Cooks: 20m | Total: 30m

NUTRITION FACTS

Calories: 496 | Carbohydrates: 30g | Fat: 30g | Protein: 19.8g | Cholesterol: 89mg

INGREDIENTS

- 3 tablespoons uncooked macaroni pasta
- 1/3 cup shredded Cheddar cheese
- 1 tablespoon butter
- 1/8 teaspoon ground mustard
- 1 tablespoon all-purpose flour

- 1 dash Worcestershire sauce
- 1/4 teaspoon salt
- 1 dash hot sauce
- 1 pinch pepper
- 1 teaspoon bread crumbs
- 1/8 teaspoon onion powder
- 1 tablespoon shredded Cheddar cheese
- 1/2 cup milk

DIRECTIONS

1. Preheat an oven to 400 degrees F (200 degrees C). Grease an oven-proof soup crock or 1 cup baking dish.
2. Fill a small saucepan with water, and bring to a boil. Stir in the macaroni; boil until cooked but still firm to the bite, about 8 minutes. Drain well, and reserve.
3. In the same saucepan, melt the butter over medium-high heat. Stir in the flour, salt, pepper, onion powder, and milk; whisk until smooth. Cook, stirring, for 2 minutes. Reduce heat to low, and whisk in 1/3 cup cheese, mustard, Worcestershire sauce, and hot sauce. Stir in the cooked macaroni. Spoon the macaroni and cheese into the prepared dish. Sprinkle with bread crumbs and 1 tablespoon cheddar cheese.
4. Bake, uncovered, until the cheese is melted and the macaroni is heated through, about 10 minutes.

LEBANESE-STYLE RED LENTIL SOUP

Servings: 8 | Prep: 20m | Cooks: 30m | Total: 50m

NUTRITION FACTS

Calories: 276 | Carbohydrates: 39.1g | Fat: 7g | Protein: 16.7g | Cholesterol: < 1mg

INGREDIENTS

- 6 cups chicken stock
- 1 tablespoon ground cumin
- 1 pound red lentils
- 1/2 teaspoon cayenne pepper
- 3 tablespoons olive oil
- 1/2 cup chopped cilantro
- 1 tablespoon minced garlic
- 3/4 cup fresh lemon juice
- 1 large onion, chopped

DIRECTIONS

1. Bring chicken stock and lentils to a boil in a large saucepan over high heat, then reduce heat to medium-low, cover, and simmer for 20 minutes.
2. Meanwhile, heat olive oil in a skillet over medium heat. Stir in garlic and onion, and cook until the onion has softened and turned translucent, about 3 minutes.
3. Stir onions into the lentils and season with cumin and cayenne. Continue simmering until the lentils are tender, about 10 minutes.
4. Carefully puree the soup in a standing blender, or with a stick blender until smooth. Stir in cilantro and lemon juice before serving.

CREAMY CUCUMBER SALAD

Servings: 8 | Prep: 10m | Cooks: 3h | Total: 3h10m

NUTRITION FACTS

Calories: 320 | Carbohydrates: 6.9g | Fat: 32.9g | Protein: 1.1g | Cholesterol: 16mg

INGREDIENTS

- 2 large cucumbers, peeled and thinly sliced
- 1 tablespoon white sugar
- 1 sweet onion, thinly sliced
- 1 teaspoon dried dill weed
- 1 tablespoon sea salt
- 1 teaspoon garlic powder
- 1 1/2 cups mayonnaise, or more to taste
- 1 teaspoon ground black pepper
- 2 tablespoons vinegar

DIRECTIONS

1. Mix cucumbers, sweet onion, and sea salt together in a bowl. Cover bowl with plastic wrap and let sit for 30 minutes.
2. Turn cucumber mixture into a colander set over a bowl or in a sink; let drain, stirring occasionally, until most of the liquid has drained, about 30 minutes more. Transfer drained cucumber mixture to a large bowl.
3. Stir mayonnaise, vinegar, sugar, dill, garlic powder, and black pepper together in a bowl with a whisk until smooth; pour over the cucumber mixture and stir to coat vegetables with the dressing.
4. Cover bowl with plastic wrap and refrigerate at least 2 hours.

CHAKCHOUKA (SHAKSHOUKA)

Servings: 4 | Prep: 20m | Cooks: 20m | Total: 40m

NUTRITION FACTS

Calories: 209 | Carbohydrates: 12.9g | Fat: 15g | Protein: 7.8g | Cholesterol: 164mg

INGREDIENTS

- 3 tablespoons olive oil
- 1 teaspoon ground cumin
- 1 1/3 cups chopped onion
- 1 teaspoon paprika
- 1 cup thinly sliced bell peppers, any color
- 1 teaspoon salt
- 2 cloves garlic, minced, or to taste
- 1 hot chile pepper, seeded and finely chopped, or to taste
- 2 1/2 cups chopped tomatoes
- 4 eggs

DIRECTIONS

1. Heat the olive oil in a skillet over medium heat. Stir in the onion, bell peppers, and garlic; cook and stir until the vegetables have softened and the onion has turned translucent, about 5 minutes.
2. Combine the tomatoes, cumin, paprika, salt, and chile pepper into a bowl and mix briefly. Pour the tomato mixture into the skillet, and stir to combine.
3. Simmer, uncovered, until the tomato juices have cooked off, about 10 minutes. Make four indentations in the tomato mixture for the eggs. Crack the eggs into the indentations. Cover the skillet and let the eggs cook until they're firm but not dry, about 5 minutes.

SPICY SWEET POTATO AND COCONUT SOUP

Servings: 6 | Prep: 10m | Cooks: 55m | Total: 1h5m

NUTRITION FACTS

Calories: 306 | Carbohydrates: 30.6g | Fat: 20g | Protein: 4.1g | Cholesterol: 0mg

INGREDIENTS

- 1 1/2 pounds orange-fleshed sweet potatoes
- 3 cups vegetable broth
- 1 tablespoon vegetable oil
- 3 1/2 tablespoons lemon juice
- 1 onion, chopped
- 1 teaspoon sea salt
- 1 (2 inch) piece fresh ginger root, thinly sliced
- 1 tablespoon toasted sesame oil
- 1 tablespoon red curry paste
- 1/2 cup chopped fresh cilantro

- 1 (15 ounce) can unsweetened coconut milk

DIRECTIONS

1. Preheat the oven to 400 degrees F (200 degrees C). Place the sweet potatoes directly on the rack and bake until tender enough to easily pierce with a fork, about 45 minutes. Remove from the oven and allow to cool.
2. Heat the oil in a large saucepan or soup pot over medium heat. Add the onion and ginger; cook and stir until tender, about 5 minutes. Stir in the curry paste and heat for 1 minute, then whisk in the coconut milk and vegetable broth. Bring to a boil, then reduce heat to low and simmer for about 5 minutes.
3. Remove the skins from the sweet potatoes and cut into bite size chunks. Add to the soup and cook for 5 more minutes so they can soak up the flavor. Stir in lemon juice and season with salt. Ladle into bowls and garnish with a drizzle of sesame oil and a little bit of cilantro.

SHRIMP AND GRITS

Servings: 4 | Prep: 25m | Cooks: 30m | Total: 55m

NUTRITION FACTS

Calories: 434 | Carbohydrates: 33.2g | Fat: 19.5g | Protein: 30.1g | Cholesterol: 226mg

INGREDIENTS

- 4 slices bacon, cut into 1/4-inch pieces
- 1 pound shrimp, peeled and deveined
- 1/4 cup water
- ½ teaspoon Cajun seasoning
- 2 tablespoons heavy whipping cream
- ½ teaspoon salt, or to taste
- 2 teaspoons lemon juice
- ¼ teaspoon ground black pepper
- 1 dash Worcestershire sauce
- 1 pinch cayenne pepper
- 4 cups water
- 1 tablespoon minced jalapeno pepper
- 2 tablespoons butter
- 2 tablespoons minced green onion
- 1 teaspoon salt
- 3 cloves garlic, minced
- 1 cup white grits
- 1 tablespoon chopped fresh parsley
- 1/2 cup shredded white Cheddar cheese

DIRECTIONS

1. Place bacon in a large skillet and cook over medium-high heat, turning occasionally, until almost crisp, 5 to 7 minutes. Remove from heat and transfer bacon to a dish, leaving drippings in the skillet.
2. Whisk 1/4 cup water, cream, lemon juice, and Worcestershire sauce together in a bowl.
3. Stir 4 cups water, butter, and 1 teaspoon salt together in a pot; bring to a boil. Whisk grits into pot, bring to a simmer, reduce heat to low, and cook until grits are creamy, 20 to 25 minutes. Remove from heat and stir white Cheddar cheese into grits.
4. Place shrimp in a large bowl and season with Cajun seasoning, 1/2 teaspoon salt, black pepper, and a pinch of cayenne pepper.
5. Heat skillet with bacon drippings over high heat. Cook shrimp in hot bacon fat in a single layer for 1 minute. Turn shrimp and add jalapeno; cook until fragrant, about 30 seconds. Stir cream mixture, bacon, green onion, and garlic to shrimp mixture; cook and stir, adding water as necessary to thin the sauce, until shrimp are cooked through, 3 to 4 minutes. Remove from heat and stir in parsley.
6. Ladle grits into a bowl and top with shrimp and sauce.

SIMPLE STROMBOLI

Servings: 3 | Prep: 10m | Cooks: 30m | Total: 40m

NUTRITION FACTS

Calories: 1065 | Carbohydrates: 77.8g | Fat: 54.6g | Protein: 59g | Cholesterol: 162mg

INGREDIENTS

- 1/2 pound bulk pork sausage (optional)
- 4 slices American cheese
- 1 (1 pound) loaf frozen bread dough, thawed
- 1 cup shredded mozzarella cheese
- 4 slices hard salami
- salt and ground black pepper to taste
- 4 slices thinly sliced ham
- 1 egg white, lightly beaten

DIRECTIONS

1. Preheat oven to 425 degrees F (220 degrees C).
2. Heat a large skillet over medium-high heat; cook and stir sausage until crumbly, evenly browned, and no longer pink, about 10 minutes. Drain and discard any excess grease.
3. Pat out bread dough on an ungreased baking sheet, to 3/4-inch thickness. Lay salami, ham, and American cheese slices in center of dough. Sprinkle with mozzarella cheese, salt, pepper, and

cooked sausage. Wrap dough to cover ingredients, pinching and sealing edges to prevent leakage; brush top with egg white.
4. Bake in preheated oven until dough is baked and lightly browned, 17 to 20 minutes.

SUN-DRIED TOMATO BASIL ORZO
Servings: 8 | Prep: 15m | Cooks: 8m | Total: 23m

NUTRITION FACTS

Calories: 255 | Carbohydrates: 38.8g | Fat: 6.9g | Protein: 10g | Cholesterol: 7mg

INGREDIENTS

- 2 cups uncooked orzo pasta
- 3/4 cup grated Parmesan cheese
- 1/2 cup chopped fresh basil leaves
- 1/2 teaspoon salt
- 1/3 cup chopped oil-packed sun-dried tomatoes
- 1/2 teaspoon ground black pepper
- 2 tablespoons olive oil

DIRECTIONS

1. Bring a large pot of lightly salted water to a boil. Add orzo and cook for 8 to 10 minutes or until al dente. Drain and set aside.
2. Place basil leaves and sun-dried tomatoes in a food processor. Pulse 4 or 5 times until blended.
3. In a large bowl, toss together the orzo, basil-tomato mixture, olive oil, Parmesan cheese, salt and pepper. Serve warm or chilled.

SPICED BUTTERNUT SQUASH SOUP
Servings: 8 | Prep: 45m | Cooks: 20m | Total: 1h5m

NUTRITION FACTS

Calories: 298 | Carbohydrates: 45.2g | Fat: 10.6g | Protein: 7.1g | Cholesterol: 34mg

INGREDIENTS

- 3 pounds butternut squash, halved and seeded
- 1/8 teaspoon ground allspice
- 2 tablespoons butter
- 1/8 teaspoon ground nutmeg
- 1 medium onion, sliced

- 1/8 teaspoon ground ginger
- 1 leek, sliced
- salt and pepper to taste
- 2 cloves garlic, sliced
- 1/2 cup sherry wine
- 2 (49.5 fluid ounce) cans chicken broth
- 1 cup half-and-half cream
- 2 large russet potatoes, peeled and quartered
- 1/2 cup sour cream (optional)
- 1/8 teaspoon cayenne pepper

DIRECTIONS

1. Preheat the oven to 375 degrees F (190 degrees C). Pour a thin layer of water in a baking dish, or a cookie sheet with sides. Place the squash halves cut side down on the dish. Bake for about 40 minutes, or until a fork can easily pierce the flesh. Cool slightly, then remove the peel. Set aside.
2. Melt the butter in a large pot over medium heat. Add the onion, leek and garlic, and saute for a few minutes, until tender. Pour the chicken broth into the pot. Add the potatoes, and bring to a boil. Cook for about 20 minutes, or until soft. Add the squash, and mash with the potatoes until chunks are small. Use an immersible hand blender to puree the soup, or transfer to a blender or food processor in batches, and puree until smooth. Return to the pot.
3. Season the soup with cayenne pepper, allspice, nutmeg, ginger, salt and pepper, then stir in the sherry and half-and-half cream. Heat through, but do not boil. Ladle into bowls, and top with a dollop of sour cream.

KRISTA'S STICKY HONEY GARLIC WINGS

Servings: 8 | Prep: 10m | Cooks: 50m | Total: 1h

NUTRITION FACTS

Calories: 337 | Carbohydrates: 35.1g | Fat: 13.4g | Protein: 19.1g | Cholesterol: 58mg

INGREDIENTS

- 24 chicken wings, split and tips discarded
- 5 tablespoons honey
- 3/4 cup packed brown sugar
- 1/4 cup reduced-sodium soy sauce
- 5 cloves garlic, minced
- 3 tablespoons cornstarch
- 1 teaspoon minced fresh ginger root
- 3/4 cup water
- 2 1/2 cups water

DIRECTIONS

1. Preheat an oven to 375 degrees F (190 degrees C).
2. Arrange the chicken wings on a baking sheet; bake until crisp, 35 to 45 minutes. Transfer the wings to a baking dish.
3. Mix together the brown sugar, garlic, ginger, 2 1/2 cups water, honey, and soy sauce in a saucepan over medium-high heat; bring to a boil. Whisk together the cornstarch and 3/4 cup water in a small bowl; stir into the sauce mixture until thickened; pour over the chicken wings to coat.
4. Return wings to oven and bake until the sauce is bubbling and the chicken is no longer pink at the bone and the juices run clear, 15 to 20 minutes.

DARRA'S FAMOUS TUNA WALDORF SALAD SANDWICH FILLING

Servings: 4 | Prep: 15m | Cooks: 5m | Total: 20m

NUTRITION FACTS

Calories: 695 | Carbohydrates: 42.4g | Fat: 48.9g | Protein: 23.1g | Cholesterol: 91mg

INGREDIENTS

- 1/2 cup mayonnaise
- 1/4 cup chopped walnuts
- 1 tablespoon prepared Dijon-style mustard
- 1/2 cup diced celery
- 1/4 teaspoon curry powder
- 1 teaspoon sweet pickle relish
- salt and pepper to taste
- 4 large croissants
- 1 (5 ounce) can tuna, drained
- 4 leaves lettuce
- 1 shallot, finely chopped
- 4 slices Swiss cheese
- 1 Granny Smith apple, cored and diced

DIRECTIONS

1. In a medium bowl, whisk together the mayonnaise, mustard, curry powder, salt and pepper. Add tuna, shallot, apple, walnuts, celery and pickle relish and toss until all ingredients are coated with dressing.

2. Lightly toast the croissants. Split in half, place a lettuce leaf on the bottom half of the croissant and fill with tuna salad. Top with a slice of Swiss cheese and the top half of the croissant. Serve with a dill pickle and potato chips. Bon appetit!

CHEESY POTATO SALAD

Servings: 6 | Prep: 15m | Cooks: 15m | Total: 30m

NUTRITION FACTS

Calories: 497 | Carbohydrates: 46.5g | Fat: 30.7g | Protein: 11.1g | Cholesterol: 49mg

INGREDIENTS

- 2 1/2 pounds red potatoes, cubed
- 1/2 bunch green onions, chopped
- 1 cup sour cream
- 1 cup shredded Cheddar cheese
- 1/2 cup mayonnaise
- 1 tablespoon real bacon bits
- 1/4 cup white sugar

DIRECTIONS

1. Place the potatoes into a pot, and fill with enough water to cover. Bring to a boil, and cook for about 10 minutes, or until easily pierced with a fork. Drain, and set aside to cool.
2. In a large bowl, mix together the sour cream, mayonnaise, sugar, half of the onions, and half of the cheese. Gently stir in the cooled potatoes. Top with remaining cheese and onions, and sprinkle bacon bits over the top.

THAI CURRY SOUP

Servings: 4 | Prep: 15m | Cooks: 35m | Total: 50m

NUTRITION FACTS

Calories: 247 | Carbohydrates: 23.8g | Fat: 13.1g | Protein: 8.2g | Cholesterol: 30mg

INGREDIENTS

- 2 ounces rice noodles (pad thai noodles)
- 1 tablespoon white sugar
- 1 tablespoon olive oil
- 1 (13.5 ounce) can reduced-fat coconut milk

- 1 clove garlic, minced
- 1/2 cup peeled and deveined medium shrimp
- 1 1/2 tablespoons minced lemon grass
- 1/2 cup sliced mushrooms
- 1 teaspoon ground ginger
- 1 (10 ounce) bag baby spinach leaves
- 2 teaspoons red curry paste
- 2 tablespoons fresh lime juice
- 1 (32 ounce) carton chicken broth
- 1/4 cup chopped cilantro
- 2 tablespoons soy sauce
- 2 green onions, thinly sliced

DIRECTIONS

1. Bring a large pot of lightly salted water to a boil. Add rice noodles and cook until al dente, about 3 minutes. Drain and rinse well with cold water to stop the cooking; set aside.
2. Heat oil in a large saucepan over medium heat. Stir in garlic, lemon grass, and ginger; cook and stir until aromatic, 30 to 60 seconds. Add the curry paste, and cook 30 seconds more. Pour in about 1/2 cup of the chicken broth, and stir until the curry paste has dissolved, then pour in the remaining chicken stock along with the soy sauce and sugar. Bring to a boil, then reduce heat to medium-low, partially cover, and simmer 20 minutes.
3. Stir in coconut milk, shrimp, mushrooms, spinach, lime juice, and cilantro. Increase heat to medium-high, and simmer until the shrimp turn pink and are no longer translucent, about 5 minutes.
4. To serve, place some rice noodles into each serving bowl and ladle soup on top of them. Garnish each bowl with a sprinkle of sliced green onion.

SOUTHERN DILL POTATO SALAD

Servings: 8 | Prep: 20m | Cooks: 20m | Total: 1h10m

NUTRITION FACTS

Calories: 279 | Carbohydrates: 10.8g | Fat: 24.1g | Protein: 5.9g | Cholesterol: 134mg

INGREDIENTS

- 10 unpeeled red potatoes
- 1/2 white onion, finely chopped
- 5 hard boiled eggs, roughly chopped
- 1 stalk celery, finely chopped
- 3/4 cup sour cream
- 1 teaspoon celery salt
- 3/4 cup mayonnaise
- salt and black pepper to taste

- 1 tablespoon apple cider vinegar, or to taste
- 1 tablespoon dried dill weed
- 1 tablespoon Dijon mustard, or to taste

DIRECTIONS

1. Place the potatoes in a large pot, cover them with water, and bring to a boil over high heat. Reduce the heat to medium-low, and simmer until the potatoes are cooked through but still firm, about 20 minutes. Remove from the water, let cool, and cut the potatoes into chunks. Set the potatoes aside.
2. In a bowl, stir together the sour cream, mayonnaise, apple cider vinegar, Dijon mustard, onion, celery, celery salt, and salt and pepper until well mixed.
3. Place the potatoes and eggs in a large salad bowl, and sprinkle with dried dill. Pour the dressing over the potatoes and eggs, and mix lightly. Cover and refrigerate the salad for at least 30 minutes. Serve cold.

CREAM OF CARROT SOUP

Servings: 8 | Prep: 20m | Cooks: 40m | Total: 1h15m

NUTRITION FACTS

Calories: 169 | Carbohydrates: 14.8g | Fat: 11.7g | Protein: 2.3g | Cholesterol: 38mg

INGREDIENTS

- 1/4 cup butter, cubed
- 1 teaspoon ground ginger
- 2 1/2 cups sliced carrots
- 1/2 cup heavy whipping cream
- 1 large potato, peeled and cubed
- 1 teaspoon curry powder
- 1 cup chopped onion
- 1/2 teaspoon salt
- 1 stalk celery, chopped
- 1/8 teaspoon ground black pepper
- 3 cups chicken broth

DIRECTIONS

1. Heat butter in a Dutch oven over medium heat; add carrots, potato, onion, celery, chicken broth, and ginger. Cover and cook, stirring occasionally, until vegetables are tender, about 30 minutes. Uncover and cool for 15 minutes.
2. Transfer soup in batches to a food processor; blend until smooth. Return soup to the Dutch oven; stir in cream. Add curry powder, salt, and black pepper; cook over low heat until heated through, about 10 minutes.

SLOW COOKER SPICY CHICKEN

Servings: 3 | Prep: 15m | Cooks: 4h | Total: 4h15m

NUTRITION FACTS

Calories: 152 | Carbohydrates: 7.1g | Fat: 2.8g | Protein: 24.4g | Cholesterol: 61mg

INGREDIENTS

- 3 skinless, boneless chicken breast halves
- 1 small red onion, chopped
- 1/2 (8 ounce) jar medium salsa
- 1 teaspoon ground cumin
- 1/4 cup tomato sauce
- 1 teaspoon chili powder
- 2 cloves garlic, minced
- 1 pinch salt and fresh ground pepper to taste

DIRECTIONS

1. Arrange the chicken breasts in the bottom of a slow cooker, and pour in the salsa and tomato sauce. Add the garlic and onion, and sprinkle in the cumin, chili powder, salt, and pepper. Set the cooker on Low, and cook until the chicken is very tender, 4 to 5 hours. Shred the chicken with two forks for serving.

MEXICAN BEAN AND RICE SALAD

Servings: 10 | Prep: 20m | Cooks: 1h | Total: 1h20m

NUTRITION FACTS

Calories: 124 | Carbohydrates: 26g | Fat: 1g | Protein: 4.7g | Cholesterol: 0mg

INGREDIENTS

- 2 cups cooked brown rice
- 2 jalapeno peppers, seeded and diced
- 1 (15 ounce) can kidney beans, rinsed and drained
- 1 lime, zested and juiced
- 1 (15 ounce) can black beans, rinsed and drained
- 1/4 cup chopped cilantro leaves
- 1 (15.25 ounce) can whole kernel corn, drained
- 1 teaspoon minced garlic
- 1 small onion, diced

- 1 1/2 teaspoons ground cumin
- 1 green bell pepper, diced
- salt to taste

DIRECTIONS

1. In a large salad bowl, combine the brown rice, kidney beans, black beans, corn, onion, green pepper, jalapeno peppers, lime zest and juice, cilantro, garlic, and cumin. Lightly toss all ingredients to mix well, and sprinkle with salt to taste.
2. Refrigerate salad for 1 hour, toss again, and serve.

CLASSIC LASAGNA

Servings: 10 | Prep: 15m | Cooks: 1h45m | Total: 2h

NUTRITION FACTS

Calories: 647 | Carbohydrates: 31.2g | Fat: 41.4g | Protein: 38.8g | Cholesterol: 174mg

INGREDIENTS

- 9 lasagna noodles
- 1/4 teaspoon dried basil
- 1 tablespoon olive oil
- 4 (15 ounce) cans tomato sauce
- 1 pound ground beef
- salt and pepper to taste
- 1 pound bulk Italian sausage
- 1 (15 ounce) container ricotta cheese
- 1 (16 ounce) can sliced mushrooms, drained
- 3 eggs, beaten
- 1 teaspoon garlic salt
- 1/3 cup grated Parmesan cheese
- 1 teaspoon dried oregano
- 1 pound shredded mozzarella cheese
- 1/2 teaspoon dried thyme

DIRECTIONS

1. Preheat oven to 350 degrees F (175 degrees C).
2. Bring a large pot of lightly salted water to a boil. Add the lasagna noodles and olive oil; cook until al dente, 8 to 10 minutes; drain.

3. Cook the ground beef and sausage in a large pot over medium heat; drain. Stir in the mushrooms, garlic salt, oregano, thyme, basil, and tomato sauce. Season with salt and pepper; simmer 30 minutes.
4. Meanwhile, mix together the ricotta cheese, eggs, and Parmesan cheese in a bowl.
5. Ladle enough of the meat sauce into a 9x13 inch baking dish to cover the bottom in a thin layer. Form a layer atop the sauce with 3 of the lasagna noodles. Spread about 1/4 of the ricotta cheese mixture over the noodles. Sprinkle about 1/3 of the mozzarella cheese over the ricotta cheese mixture and then ladle about 1/3 of the meat sauce over the mozzarella cheese. Repeat layering twice more, topping with the remaining 1/4 pound of mozzarella cheese.
6. Bake in preheated oven 90 minutes. Allow to sit 10 to 15 minutes before serving.

BUFFALO CHICKEN WRAPS
Servings: 4 | Prep: 20m | Cooks: 10m | Total: 30m

NUTRITION FACTS

Calories: 588 | Carbohydrates: 39.8g | Fat: 32.6g | Protein: 30.4g | Cholesterol: 83mg

INGREDIENTS

- 1 tablespoon vegetable oil
- 4 (10 inch) flour tortillas
- 1 tablespoon butter
- 2 cups shredded lettuce
- 1 pound skinless, boneless chicken breasts, cut into bite-size pieces
- 1 celery stalk, diced
- 1/4 cup hot sauce
- 1/2 cup blue cheese dressing

DIRECTIONS

1. Heat the vegetable oil and butter in a large skillet over medium-high heat. Place the chicken in the pan; cook and stir until the chicken is no longer pink in the center and the juices run clear, about 10 minutes. Remove the pan from the heat. Pour the hot sauce over the cooked chicken and toss to coat.
2. Lay out the flour tortillas and divide the chicken evenly among the tortillas. Top the chicken with lettuce, celery, and blue cheese dressing. Fold in the sides of the tortilla and roll the wrap burrito-style.

SESAME NOODLE SALAD
Servings: 8 | Prep: 15m | Cooks: 5m | Total: 20m

NUTRITION FACTS

Calories: 338 | Carbohydrates: 40.8g | Fat: 16.8g | Protein: 7.3g | Cholesterol: 0mg

INGREDIENTS

- 1 (16 ounce) package angel hair pasta
- 1/4 cup white sugar
- 1/2 cup sesame oil
- 1 teaspoon sesame seeds, or more if desired
- 1/2 cup soy sauce
- 1 green onion, chopped
- 1/4 cup balsamic vinegar
- 1 red bell pepper, diced
- 1 tablespoon hot chili oil

DIRECTIONS

1. Fill a large pot with lightly salted water and bring to a rolling boil over high heat. Once the water is boiling, stir in the angel hair pasta, and return to a boil. Cook the pasta uncovered, stirring occasionally, until the pasta has cooked through, but is still firm to the bite, 4 to 5 minutes. Drain well in a colander set in the sink.
2. Whisk together the sesame oil, soy sauce, balsamic vinegar, chili oil, and sugar in a large bowl. Toss the pasta in the dressing, then sprinkle with sesame seeds, green onion, and bell pepper. Serve warm, or cover and refrigerate for a cold salad.

TUNA MELTS

Servings: 8 | Prep: 15m | Cooks: 10m | Total: 25m

NUTRITION FACTS

Calories: 483 | Carbohydrates: 34.1g | Fat: 27.7g | Protein: 24.5g | Cholesterol: 41mg

INGREDIENTS

- 1 (1 pound) loaf French bread
- 2 cups mozzarella cheese, shredded
- 1 small sweet onion, peeled and diced
- 1 cup mayonnaise
- 1 (12 ounce) can tuna, drained

DIRECTIONS

1. Preheat oven to 350 degrees F (175 degrees C).

2. In a mixing bowl, combine sweet onion, drained tuna, mozzarella, and mayonnaise. Mix thoroughly.
3. Spread tuna mixture on slices of French bread to form a sandwich. Place sandwiches on a cookie sheet.
4. Bake in a preheated oven for 10 minutes.

TOMATO BASIL SOUP

Servings: 8 | Prep: 25m | Cooks: 30m | Total: 55m

NUTRITION FACTS

Calories: 270 | Carbohydrates: 10.1g | Fat: 25.4g | Protein: 3g | Cholesterol: 84mg

INGREDIENTS

- 6 tablespoons butter
- 1 (8 ounce) can tomato sauce (such as Hunt's)
- 1 onion, thinly sliced
- 1 1/4 cups chicken broth
- 15 baby carrots, thinly sliced
- 2 tablespoons chopped fresh basil
- 2 stalks celery, thinly sliced
- 1 tablespoon chopped fresh oregano
- 3 cloves garlic, chopped
- salt and ground black pepper to taste
- 1 (28 ounce) can tomato sauce (such as Hunt's)
- 1 1/2 cups heavy whipping cream

DIRECTIONS

1. Melt butter in a large pot over medium-low heat; cook and stir onion, carrots, celery, and garlic until vegetables are tender, about 10 minutes. Stir in both amounts of tomato sauce, chicken broth, basil, and oregano. Increase heat to medium and simmer until soup is reduced, 10 to 20 minutes.
2. Pour soup into a blender no more than half full. Cover and hold lid down; pulse a few times before leaving on to blend. Add cream. Continue to puree in batches until smooth, transferring creamy soup to another pot.
3. Heat soup over medium-high heat until hot, about 5 minutes more.

BEST BEAN SALAD

Servings: 18 | Prep: 20m | Cooks: 8h | Total: 8h20m

NUTRITION FACTS

Calories: 167 | Carbohydrates: 23.6g | Fat: 6.5g | Protein: 4.4g | Cholesterol: 0mg

INGREDIENTS

- 1 (14.5 ounce) can green beans, drained
- 1/2 cup chopped celery
- 1 (14.5 ounce) can wax beans, drained
- 1/2 cup salad oil
- 1 (15.5 ounce) can garbanzo beans, drained
- 1/2 cup vinegar
- 1 (14.5 ounce) can kidney beans, drained
- 1/2 teaspoon salt
- 1 (14.5 ounce) can black beans, drained
- 1/2 teaspoon ground black pepper
- 1/2 cup chopped green pepper
- 3/4 cup white sugar
- 1/2 cup chopped onion

DIRECTIONS

1. Combine the green beans, wax beans, garbanzo beans, kidney beans, green pepper, onion, and celery in a large bowl; toss to mix.
2. Whisk together the oil, vinegar, salt, pepper, and sugar in a separate bowl until the sugar is dissolved; pour over the bean mixture. Refrigerate 8 hours or overnight before serving.

GOURMET CHICKEN SANDWICH

Servings: 4 | Prep: 10m | Cooks: 15m | Total: 25m

NUTRITION FACTS

Calories: 522 | Carbohydrates: 58g | Fat: 15.7g | Protein: 34.6g | Cholesterol: 70mg

INGREDIENTS

- 4 skinless, boneless chicken breast halves - pounded to 1/4 inch thickness
- 2 tablespoons mayonnaise
- ground black pepper to taste
- 2 teaspoons prepared Dijon-style mustard
- 1 tablespoon olive oil
- 1 teaspoon chopped fresh rosemary
- 1 teaspoon minced garlic
- 8 slices garlic and rosemary focaccia bread

DIRECTIONS

1. Sprinkle pepper on one side of each chicken cutlet. Heat oil in a large skillet; brown garlic in oil, then add chicken, pepper-side-down. Saute chicken until cooked through and juices run clear, about 12 to 15 minutes.
2. In a small bowl combine the mayonnaise, mustard and rosemary. Mix together and spread mixture on 4 slices focaccia bread. Place 1 chicken cutlet on each of these slices, then top each with another bread slice.

JAN'S PRETZEL DOGS
Servings: 18 | Prep: 35m | Cooks: 35m | Total: 2h10m

NUTRITION FACTS

Calories: 299 | Carbohydrates: 27.2g | Fat: 15.8g | Protein: 9.7g | Cholesterol: 41mg

INGREDIENTS

- 1 (12 fluid ounce) can or bottle room temperature beer
- 1 large egg yolk
- 1 tablespoon white sugar
- 1 tablespoon water
- 2 teaspoons kosher salt
- 10 cups water
- 1 (.25 ounce) package active dry yeast
- 2/3 cup baking soda
- 4 1/2 cups bread flour
- 1/4 cup kosher salt, divided - or to taste
- 1/4 cup unsalted butter, melted
- 18 hot dogs

DIRECTIONS

1. Heat the beer in a saucepan over low heat until it reaches 110 degrees F (45 degrees C).
2. Combine the warm beer, sugar, and 2 teaspoons kosher salt in a bowl. Sprinkle the yeast on top, and let stand for 5 minutes until the yeast softens and begins to form a creamy foam.
3. Place the bread flour and butter in a bread machine. Add the yeast mixture, then select the dough cycle.
4. Preheat an oven to 450 degrees F (230 degrees C).
5. Line 2 baking sheets with parchment paper or grease with vegetable oil.
6. Beat the egg yolk in a small bowl with 1 tablespoon water; set aside.
7. Stir baking soda into 10 cups water in a large pot until dissolved, and bring to a boil.
8. Turn the dough out onto a lightly-oiled surface, and roll into a 10x20-inch rectangle.
9. Cut the dough into 18 1-inch wide strips, then wrap each strip tightly around a hot dog in a spiral, pinching the edges to seal, and leaving the ends open. About half an inch of hot dog should peek out of each end of the dough wrapper.

10. Drop 2 or 3 dough-wrapped hot dogs into the boiling water for 30 seconds.
11. Arrange the boiled hot dogs on the prepared baking sheets. Brush each pretzel dog with the egg yolk mixture, and sprinkle with the remaining 1/4 cup salt.
12. Bake in the preheated oven until golden brown, about 15 minutes.

SOUTHERN FRIED CABBAGE WITH BACON, MUSHROOMS, AND ONIONS

Servings: 10 | Prep: 15m | Cooks: 30m | Total: 45m

NUTRITION FACTS

Calories: 123 | Carbohydrates: 9.6g | Fat: 6.4g | Protein: 8g | Cholesterol: 16mg

INGREDIENTS

- 1 pound bacon
- 1 (8 ounce) package sliced fresh mushrooms
- 1 large head cabbage, chopped
- salt and ground black pepper to taste
- 1 large onion, chopped

DIRECTIONS

1. Place bacon in a large skillet and cook over medium-high heat, turning occasionally, until evenly browned, about 10 minutes. Drain the bacon slices on paper towels; crumble when cooled. Drain all but 3 tablespoons of bacon drippings from skillet.
2. Cook and stir cabbage, onion, and mushrooms in the remaining bacon drippings until tender and lightly browned, about 20 minutes. Fold bacon into cabbage mixture. Season with salt and black pepper.

TANGY TURKEY AND SWISS SANDWICHES

Servings: 4 | Prep: 15m | Cooks: 10m | Total: 25m

NUTRITION FACTS

Calories: 856 | Carbohydrates: 42.6g | Fat: 58.9g | Protein: 41.9g | Cholesterol: 154mg

INGREDIENTS

- 3/4 cup chopped red onion
- 6 tablespoons butter, softened
- 1 tablespoon dried thyme

- 1 pound thinly sliced roast turkey
- 1/2 cup mayonnaise
- 8 slices tomato
- 1/4 cup coarse-grain brown mustard
- 8 slices Swiss cheese
- 8 slices country style French Bread

DIRECTIONS

1. In a small bowl, stir together the red onion, thyme, mayonnaise and mustard. Spread some of this mixture onto one side of each slice of bread. Spread butter onto the other side of the slices of bread.
2. Heat a large skillet over medium heat. Place 4 slices of the bread into the skillet with the butter side down. On each slice of bread, layer 1/4 of the sliced turkey, then 2 slices of tomato, and top with 2 slices of Swiss cheese. Place remaining slices of bread over the top with the butter side up. When the bottoms of the sandwiches are golden brown, flip over, and cook until golden on the other side.

BLT WRAPS

Servings: 4 | Prep: 15m | Cooks: 10m | Total: 25m

NUTRITION FACTS

Calories: 695 | Carbohydrates: 64.2g | Fat: 34.1g | Protein: 31.4g | Cholesterol: 71mg

INGREDIENTS

- 1 pound thick sliced bacon, cut into 1 inch pieces
- 1/2 head iceberg lettuce, shredded
- 4 (12 inch) flour tortillas
- 1 tomato, diced
- 1 cup shredded Cheddar cheese

DIRECTIONS

1. Place bacon in a large, deep skillet. Cook over medium-high heat until evenly brown. Drain, and set aside.
2. Place 1 tortilla on a microwave-safe plate. Sprinkle tortilla with 1/4 cup cheese. Cook in microwave 1 to 2 minutes, or until cheese is melted. Immediately top with 1/4 of the bacon, lettuce, and tomato. Fold sides of tortilla over, then roll up. Repeat with remaining ingredients. Cut each wrap in half before serving.

BEEF CHIMICHANGAS

Servings: 6 | Prep: 15m | Cooks: 25m | Total: 40m

NUTRITION FACTS

Calories: 369 | Carbohydrates: 15.8g | Fat: 25.4g | Protein: 19.7g | Cholesterol: 70mg

INGREDIENTS

- 1 pound ground beef
- 1 (4 ounce) can chopped green chilies
- 1 small onion, chopped
- 2 tablespoons distilled white vinegar
- 1 clove garlic, minced
- 1 cup shredded Cheddar cheese
- 1/2 teaspoon taco seasoning mix, or more to taste
- 1/4 cup margarine
- 1 teaspoon dried oregano
- 6 (7 inch) corn tortillas
- 1/4 cup sour cream

DIRECTIONS

1. Preheat oven to 450 degrees F (230 degrees C).
2. Brown the ground beef, onion, garlic, taco seasoning, and oregano in a skillet over medium heat, breaking the meat up into crumbles as it cooks, about 8 minutes. Drain off excess fat. Stir in sour cream, chilies, and vinegar until well mixed. Remove from heat, and mix in the Cheddar cheese.
3. Melt margarine in a small skillet over low heat. When melted, dip each tortilla into the margarine for about 30 seconds, or until soft. Place the softened tortilla onto a baking sheet, and fill with about 1/3 cup of the meat mixture. Fold the right and left sides of the tortilla over the filling, then the top and bottom, making an envelope that completely encloses the filling. Flip the tortilla seam side down on the baking sheet. Repeat with remaining tortillas and filling.
4. Bake in the preheated oven until the tortilla is crisp, about 15 minutes.

TURKEY WILD RICE SOUP

Servings: 8 | Prep: 20m | Cooks: 1h | Total: 1h20m

NUTRITION FACTS

Calories: 252 | Carbohydrates: 14.4g | Fat: 15.2g | Protein: 14.3g | Cholesterol: 61mg

INGREDIENTS

- 2/3 cup uncooked wild rice
- 1/3 cup shredded carrot
- 2 cups water
- 2 cups chopped cooked turkey
- 6 tablespoons butter
- 1/2 teaspoon kosher salt, or to taste
- 1/4 cup finely chopped onion
- 1/2 teaspoon ground black pepper, or to taste
- 1/4 cup finely chopped celery
- 1/4 cup chopped slivered almonds
- 1/3 cup all-purpose flour
- 1/2 teaspoon lemon juice
- 4 cups turkey broth
- 3/4 cup half-and-half cream

DIRECTIONS

1. Bring the wild rice and water to a boil in a saucepan. Reduce heat to medium-low, cover, and simmer until the rice is tender but not mushy, 40 to 45 minutes. Drain off any excess liquid, fluff the rice with a fork, and cook uncovered 5 minutes more. Set the cooked rice aside.
2. Melt the butter in a soup pot over medium heat. Cook and stir the onion and celery until the onion is translucent, about 5 minutes. Stir in the flour, and cook until it turns a pale yellowish-brown color, 3 to 5 minutes. Gradually whisk in the turkey stock until no lumps of flour remain. Stir in the carrot. Bring the mixture to a simmer, and cook, whisking constantly, until the stock is thick and smooth and the carrot is tender, about 2 more minutes.
3. Stir in the wild rice, turkey, salt, pepper, and almonds. Return to a simmer, and cook 2 more minutes to heat the ingredients. Stir in the lemon juice and half-and-half; bring the soup almost to a boil, and serve hot.

SPINACH BASIL PASTA SALAD

Servings: 10 | Prep: 15m | Cooks: 15m | Total: 30m

NUTRITION FACTS

Calories: 372 | Carbohydrates: 36.4g | Fat: 20.7g | Protein: 13.6g | Cholesterol: 15mg

INGREDIENTS

- 1 (16 ounce) package bow tie pasta
- 4 ounces prosciutto, diced
- 1 (6 ounce) package spinach leaves
- salt and ground black pepper to taste
- 2 cups fresh basil leaves
- 3/4 cup freshly grated Parmesan cheese

- 1/2 cup extra virgin olive oil
- 1/2 cup toasted pine nuts
- 3 cloves garlic, minced

DIRECTIONS

1. Fill a large pot with lightly salted water and bring to a rolling boil over high heat. Once the water is boiling, stir in the bow tie pasta and return to a boil. Cook the pasta uncovered, stirring occasionally, until the pasta has cooked through, but is still firm to the bite, about 12 minutes. Rinse with cold water to cool. Drain well in a colander set in the sink.
2. Toss the spinach and basil together in a large bowl.
3. Heat the olive oil in a skillet over medium heat; cook and stir the garlic in the hot oil for 1 minute; stir in the prosciutto and cook 2 to 3 minutes more. Remove from heat. Add to the bowl with the spinach and basil mixture; toss to combine. Pour in the drained pasta and retoss. Season with salt and pepper. Sprinkle with the Parmesan cheese and pine nuts to serve.

SPAGHETTI SQUASH WITH PINE NUTS, SAGE, AND ROMANO

Servings: 4 | Prep: 10m | Cooks: 50m | Total: 1h

NUTRITION FACTS

Calories: 150 | Carbohydrates: 13.7g | Fat: 9.4g | Protein: 5.6g | Cholesterol: 13mg

INGREDIENTS

- 1 spaghetti squash, halved lengthwise and seeded
- 2 tablespoons chopped fresh sage
- 1/4 cup toasted pine nuts
- 2 teaspoons butter, melted
- 1/4 cup grated Pecorino Romano cheese
- salt and pepper to taste

DIRECTIONS

1. Preheat oven to 350 degrees F (175 degrees C).
2. Place the squash, cut side down, in a large baking dish.
3. Bake the squash in the preheated oven for 50 minutes.
4. Scrape flesh of squash from the rind using a fork and place in a bowl. Add the pine nuts, cheese, sage, butter, salt, and pepper; toss to combine. Serve immediately.

CRESCENT DOGS

Servings: 8 | Prep: 10m | Cooks: 15m | Total: 25m

NUTRITION FACTS

Calories: 313 | Carbohydrates: 13.2g | Fat: 23.8g | Protein: 10.2g | Cholesterol: 37mg

INGREDIENTS

- 8 hot dogs
- 1 (8 ounce) can Pillsbury refrigerated crescent dinner rolls
- 4 slices American cheese, each cut into 6 strips

DIRECTIONS

1. Heat oven to 375 degrees F. Slit hot dogs to within 1/2 inch of ends; insert 3 strips of cheese into each slit.
2. Separate dough into triangles. Wrap dough triangle around each hot dog. Place on ungreased cookie sheet, cheese side up.
3. Bake 12-15 min or until golden brown.

BREAD MACHINE PUMPERNICKEL BREAD

Servings: 12 | Prep: 10m | Cooks: 3h45m | Total: 3h55m

NUTRITION FACTS

Calories: 119 | Carbohydrates: 22.4g | Fat: 2.3g | Protein: 3.4g | Cholesterol: 0mg

INGREDIENTS

- 1 1/8 cups warm water
- 1 1/2 cups bread flour
- 1 1/2 tablespoons vegetable oil
- 1 cup rye flour
- 1/3 cup molasses
- 1 cup whole wheat flour
- 3 tablespoons cocoa
- 1 1/2 tablespoons vital wheat gluten (optional)
- 1 tablespoon caraway seed (optional)
- 2 1/2 teaspoons bread machine yeast
- 1 1/2 teaspoons salt

DIRECTIONS

1. Place ingredients in the pan of the bread machine in the order recommended by the manufacturer. Select Basic cycle; press Start.

IRISH BACON AND CABBAGE SOUP

Servings: 4 | Prep: 15m | Cooks: 30m | Total: 45m

NUTRITION FACTS

Calories: 276 | Carbohydrates: 38.4g | Fat: 8.1g | Protein: 12.3g | Cholesterol: 21mg

INGREDIENTS

- 1/2 pound Irish bacon, diced
- 1 cup chicken stock, or as needed
- 2 large potatoes, peeled and cubed
- Salt and black pepper to taste
- 1 (15 ounce) can diced tomatoes with juice
- 2 cups thinly sliced dark green Savoy cabbage leaves

DIRECTIONS

1. Place bacon in a large, deep stockpot or saucepan. Cook over medium high heat until evenly brown. Drain off any excess fat.
2. Stir in potatoes, tomatoes, and enough chicken stock to cover. Season with salt and pepper. Bring to a boil, reduce heat and let simmer for 20 minutes, or until potatoes are tender.
3. Stir in cabbage and allow the soup to simmer for a few minutes longer before serving.

MEL'S CRAB SALAD

Servings: 8 | Prep: 15m | Cooks: 8h | Total: 8h15m

NUTRITION FACTS

Calories: 165 | Carbohydrates: 12.2g | Fat: 11g | Protein: 4.6g | Cholesterol: 19mg

INGREDIENTS

- 1 pound imitation crabmeat, flaked
- 1/3 cup mayonnaise (such as Hellmann's/Best Foods)
- 1/2 cup finely chopped celery, or more to taste
- 1 tablespoon white sugar
- 1/2 cup reduced-fat ranch dressing (such as Hidden Valley Ranch LIght)
- 1 teaspoon minced fresh parsley

DIRECTIONS

1. Gently mix flaked imitation crab, celery, ranch dressing, mayonnaise, sugar, and parsley in a salad bowl until thoroughly combined. Refrigerate overnight, stirring occasionally. Stir again just before serving.

GRILLED PIZZA WRAPS

Servings: 8 | Prep: 10m | Cooks: 20m | Total: 30m

NUTRITION FACTS

Calories: 543 | Carbohydrates: 40.6g | Fat: 31.9g | Protein: 22.5g | Cholesterol: 69mg

INGREDIENTS

- 2 tablespoons margarine, softened
- 1/2 cup pizza sauce
- 8 (10 inch) flour tortillas
- 4 ounces sliced pepperoni
- 1 (16 ounce) package shredded Cheddar-Monterey Jack cheese blend

DIRECTIONS

1. Heat a large skillet over medium-low heat. Spread margarine over one side of a tortilla, and place it margarine-side down in the skillet. Spoon a tablespoon of pizza sauce onto half of the tortilla. Sprinkle 1/2 cup of shredded cheese over the sauce, and top with a few slices of pepperoni. Fold the clean half of the tortilla over the filling, and cook until golden on each side. Repeat with remaining tortillas.

TOMATO GORGONZOLA SOUP

Servings: 4 | Prep: 15m | Cooks: 20m | Total: 35m

NUTRITION FACTS

Calories: 277 | Carbohydrates: 13.7g | Fat: 22.5g | Protein: 7.2g | Cholesterol: 64mg

INGREDIENTS

- 1 tablespoon olive oil
- 1/4 cup milk
- 1/4 large red onion, diced
- 1 (14.5 ounce) can diced tomatoes

- 1/2 cup red bell pepper, diced
- 1 1/2 cups tomato juice
- 2 cloves cloves garlic, minced
- 2 teaspoons dried basil
- 1/4 cup Gorgonzola cheese, crumbled
- 1 teaspoon white sugar
- 4 ounces cream cheese, softened
- 1/4 teaspoon ground white pepper
- 1/4 cup heavy cream

DIRECTIONS

1. Heat oil in a medium saucepan over medium heat. Add the onion, pepper, and garlic; cook and stir 4 to 5 minutes or until vegetables are soft.
2. Add the cheeses, cream, and milk; heat mixture until cheeses melt and the mixture is simmering.
3. Stir in the tomatoes (including their liquid), tomato juice, basil, sugar, and pepper. Continue to simmer mixture for 15 to 20 minutes while stirring constantly. Do not boil.

SPECIAL LOBSTER BISQUE

Servings: 8 | Prep: 10m | Cooks: 25m | Total: 35m

NUTRITION FACTS

Calories: 279 | Carbohydrates: 13.7g | Fat: 17.3g | Protein: 16.7g | Cholesterol: 94mg

INGREDIENTS

- 6 tablespoons butter
- 1 1/2 cups chicken stock
- 6 tablespoons all-purpose flour
- 3 tablespoons minced onion
- 1 teaspoon salt
- 3 cups cooked lobster meat, shredded
- 1/4 teaspoon ground black pepper
- 1 tablespoon paprika
- 1/2 teaspoon celery salt
- 1/2 cup light cream
- 4 1/2 cups milk

DIRECTIONS

1. Melt the butter in a large pot over medium heat. Stir in the flour, salt, pepper and celery salt until well blended. Gradually stir in the milk so that no lumps form, and then stir in the chicken stock. Cook over low heat, stirring constantly, until the soup begins to thicken. Add the onion and lobster; season with paprika. Cook and stir for 10 more minutes. Stir in the cream, heat through and serve.

BUFFALO CHICKEN CHILI

Servings: 10 | Prep: 15m | Cooks: 1h15m | Total: 1h30m

NUTRITION FACTS

Calories: 301 | Carbohydrates: 30g | Fat: 8.6g | Protein: 28.3g | Cholesterol: 61mg

INGREDIENTS

- 1 tablespoon extra-virgin olive oil
- 2 tablespoons ground cumin
- 2 tablespoons butter
- 1 tablespoon ground paprika
- 2 pounds ground chicken breast
- salt and pepper to taste
- 1 large carrot, peeled and finely chopped
- ½ cup hot buffalo wing sauce (such as Frank's REDHOT Buffalo Wing Sauce), or to taste
- 1 large onion, chopped
- 2 (15 ounce) cans tomato sauce
- 3 stalks celery, finely chopped
- 1 (15 ounce) can crushed tomatoes
- 5 cloves garlic, chopped
- 1 (15 ounce) can white kidney or cannellini beans, drained
- 5 tablespoons chili powder
- 1 (19 ounce) can red kidney beans, drained

DIRECTIONS

1. Heat olive oil and butter in a large pot over medium-high heat. Place chicken in the pot. Cook and stir 7 to 10 minutes, until chicken is no longer pink. Stir in the carrot, onion, celery, garlic, chili powder, cumin, paprika, and salt and pepper, and cook and stir until the onion is translucent and the vegetables are beginning to soften, 3 to 4 more minutes.
2. Stir in the hot sauce, tomato sauce, crushed tomatoes, and white and red kidney beans. Bring to a boil, and simmer over medium-low heat about 1 hour, until the vegetables are tender and the flavors have blended.

CRAB LEGS WITH GARLIC BUTTER SAUCE

Servings: 2 | Prep: 5m | Cooks: 15m | Total: 20m

NUTRITION FACTS

Calories: 520 | Carbohydrates: 1g | Fat: 37.5g | Protein: 43.6g | Cholesterol: 274mg

INGREDIENTS

- 1 pound Snow Crab clusters, thawed if necessary
- 1 1/2 teaspoons dried parsley
- 1/4 cup butter
- 1/8 teaspoon salt
- 1 clove garlic, minced
- 1/4 teaspoon fresh-ground black pepper

DIRECTIONS

1. Cut a slit, length-wise, into the shell of each piece of crab.
2. Melt the butter in a large skillet over medium heat; cook the garlic in the butter until translucent; stir in the parsley, salt, and pepper. Continue to heat mixture until bubbling. Add the crab legs; toss to coat; allow to simmer in the butter mixture until completely heated, 5 to 6 minutes.

COCONUT CURRY PUMPKIN SOUP

Servings: 6 | Prep: 20m | Cooks: 30m | Total: 50m

NUTRITION FACTS

Calories: 171 | Carbohydrates: 12g | Fat: 13.5g | Protein: 2g | Cholesterol: 0mg

INGREDIENTS

- 1/4 cup coconut oil
- 1/2 teaspoon salt
- 1 cup chopped onions
- 1/4 teaspoon ground coriander
- 1 clove garlic, minced
- 1/4 teaspoon crushed red pepper flakes
- 3 cups vegetable broth
- 1 (15 ounce) can 100% pure pumpkin
- 1 teaspoon curry powder
- 1 cup light coconut milk

DIRECTIONS

1. Heat the coconut oil in a deep pot over medium-high heat. Stir in the onions and garlic; cook until the onions are translucent, about 5 minutes. Mix in the vegetable broth, curry powder, salt, coriander, and red pepper flakes. Cook and stir until the mixture comes to a gentle boil, about 10 minutes. Cover, and boil 15 to 20 minutes more, stirring occasionally. Whisk in the pumpkin and coconut milk, and cook another 5 minutes.
2. Pour the soup into a blender, filling only half way and working in batches if necessary; process until smooth. Return to a pot, and reheat briefly over medium heat before serving.

ROASTED CARROT SALAD

Servings: 6 | Prep: 20m | Cooks: 30m | Total: 1h30m

NUTRITION FACTS

Calories: 295 | Carbohydrates: 23.8g | Fat: 19.7g | Protein: 7.6g | Cholesterol: 14mg

INGREDIENTS

- 2 pounds carrots, peeled and thinly sliced on the diagonal
- 1 teaspoon honey
- 1/2 cup slivered almonds
- 1 tablespoon cider vinegar
- 2 cloves garlic, minced
- 1/3 cup dried cranberries
- 1/4 cup extra-virgin olive oil
- 1 (4 ounce) package crumbled Danish blue cheese
- salt and ground black pepper to taste
- 2 cups arugula

DIRECTIONS

1. Preheat an oven to 400 degrees F (200 degrees C).
2. Combine the carrots, almonds, and garlic in a mixing bowl. Drizzle with the olive oil, then season to taste with salt and pepper. Spread out onto an ungreased baking sheet.
3. Bake the carrots in the preheated oven until soft and the edges turn brown, about 30 minutes. Remove and allow to cool to room temperature.
4. Once cool, return the carrots to the mixing bowl, and drizzle with honey and vinegar; toss until coated. Add the cranberries and blue cheese; toss again until evenly mixed. Combine with the arugula and serve immediately.

TONYA'S TERRIFIC SLOPPY JOES

Servings: 4 | Prep: 10m | Cooks: 30m | Total: 40m

NUTRITION FACTS

Calories: 362 | Carbohydrates: 31.2g | Fat: 15.3g | Protein: 23.7g | Cholesterol: 71mg

INGREDIENTS

- 2 pounds ground beef
- 1 1/2 teaspoons Worcestershire sauce
- 1/2 cup chopped onion
- 1 teaspoon vinegar
- 1/4 cup chopped celery
- 1/4 teaspoon dry mustard powder
- 7 ounces ketchup
- 1/8 teaspoon lemon juice
- 1 tablespoon brown sugar
- 8 white or wheat hamburger buns

DIRECTIONS

1. Place a large skillet over medium-high heat. Crumble ground beef into skillet; add onion and celery. Cook and stir beef mixture until beef is completely browned, 7 to 10 minutes.
2. Stir ketchup, brown sugar, Worcestershire sauce, vinegar, mustard, and lemon juice through the beef mixture. Reduce heat to medium-low and cook mixture at a simmer until mixture is hot and sauce has thickened, about 20 minutes.

JALAPENO POPPER GRILLED CHEESE SANDWICH

Servings: 2 | Prep: 10m | Cooks: 10m | Total: 20m

NUTRITION FACTS

Calories: 528 | Carbohydrates: 40.9g | Fat: 34g | Protein: 16.5g | Cholesterol: 89mg

INGREDIENTS

- 2 ounces cream cheese, softened
- 4 teaspoons butter
- 1 tablespoon sour cream
- 8 tortilla chips, crushed
- 10 pickled jalapeno pepper slices, or to taste - chopped
- 1/2 cup shredded Colby-Monterey Jack cheese
- 2 ciabatta sandwich rolls

DIRECTIONS

1. Combine the cream cheese, sour cream, and pickled jalapeno in a small bowl. Set aside. Preheat skillet over medium heat.

2. Slice each roll in half horizontally, then slice the rounded tops off the ciabatta rolls to make a flat top half. Spread 1 teaspoon butter on the doughy cut side of the bottom bun and 1 teaspoon butter on the now flattened top bun. Place half of the cream cheese mixture, half of the crushed chips, and half of the shredded cheese on the non-buttered side of the bottom bun. Place the top half of the bun on the sandwich and place the sandwich on the hot skillet. Repeat with the second sandwich.
3. Grill until lightly browned and flip over, about 3 to 5 minutes; continue grilling until cheese is melted and the second side is golden brown.

ROASTED CAULIFLOWER AND LEEK SOUP
Servings: 6 | Prep: 10m | Cooks: 1h5m | Total: 1h15m

NUTRITION FACTS

Calories: 209 | Carbohydrates: 15.4g | Fat: 15.9g | Protein: 3.8g | Cholesterol: 34mg

INGREDIENTS

- 2 cloves garlic, minced
- 1 quart chicken stock
- 2 tablespoons vegetable oil
- 1/3 cup heavy whipping cream
- 1 head cauliflower, broken into florets
- 1 teaspoon dried chervil
- 3 tablespoons butter
- 1 teaspoon kosher salt
- 2 leeks, white part only, chopped
- 1 tablespoon cracked black pepper
- 1/4 cup all-purpose flour

DIRECTIONS

1. Preheat the oven to 375 degrees F (190 degrees C).
2. Stir garlic and vegetable oil together in a small bowl. Arrange cauliflower florets on a baking sheet; pour oil mixture over cauliflower. Toss to coat.
3. Bake cauliflower in the preheated oven until tender and lightly browned, about 30 minutes.
4. Melt butter in a 4-quart stockpot over medium heat; cook and stir leeks and flour in the melted butter until fragrant and well blended, 5 to 10 minutes. Add cauliflower, chicken stock, and cream; simmer until flavors have combined, 20 to 25 minutes. Stir chervil, salt, and pepper into the soup; simmer until desired thickness, 10 to 15 more minutes.

BEAN WITH BACON

Servings: 6 | Prep: 15m | Cooks: 2h20m | Total: 2h35m

NUTRITION FACTS

Calories: 631 | Carbohydrates: 52.2g | Fat: 35.3g | Protein: 26.6g | Cholesterol: 51mg

INGREDIENTS

- 1 (16 ounce) package dried navy beans
- 1 bay leaf
- 9 cups water
- 1/3 teaspoon salt
- 1 pound bacon
- 1/4 teaspoon ground black pepper
- 2 onions, chopped
- 1/8 teaspoon ground cloves
- 2 stalks celery, chopped
- 1 (16 ounce) can diced tomatoes
- 4 teaspoons chicken bouillon
- 4 cups water

DIRECTIONS

1. Boil the beans in 9 cups of the water and then let sit for one hour. Drain and set aside.
2. Cook the bacon to your desired texture (it can be soft or crisp, whatever you prefer) and drain except for 1/4 cup grease. Coarsely chop the bacon.
3. Add the onions and celery to the reserved grease and bacon and saute until soft, do not drain. Add the chicken base or cubes, 4 cups water, beans, bay leaf, salt, pepper, and cloves, and simmer for 2 hours.
4. Stir in the tomatoes with their juice. Serve.

POTATO SALAD

Servings: 20 | Prep: 20m | Cooks: 10m | Total: 6h30m

NUTRITION FACTS

Calories: 339 | Carbohydrates: 20.4g | Fat: 27.6g | Protein: 4.1g | Cholesterol: 53mg

INGREDIENTS

- 5 pounds red potatoes, chopped
- 1/2 cup chopped celery

- 3 cups mayonnaise
- 3 tablespoons prepared mustard
- 2 cups finely chopped pickles
- 1 tablespoon apple cider vinegar
- 5 hard-cooked eggs, chopped
- 1 teaspoon salt, or to taste
- 1/2 cup chopped red onion
- 1/2 teaspoon ground black pepper

DIRECTIONS

1. Place potatoes into a large pot and cover with salted water; bring to a boil. Reduce heat to medium-low and simmer until tender, about 10 minutes. Drain. Return potatoes to empty pot to dry while you mix the dressing. Sprinkle with salt.
2. Stir mayonnaise, pickles, hard-cooked eggs, red onion, celery, mustard, cider vinegar, 1 teaspoon salt, and pepper together in a large bowl. Fold potatoes into the mayonnaise mixture. Allow to chill at least six hours, or overnight, before serving.

CAJUN SHRIMP

Servings: 4 | Prep: 5m | Cooks: 5m | Total: 10m

NUTRITION FACTS

Calories: 166 | Carbohydrates: 0.9g | Fat: 5g | Protein: 28 g | Cholesterol: 259mg

INGREDIENTS

- 1 teaspoon paprika
- 1/4 teaspoon ground black pepper
- 3/4 teaspoon dried thyme
- 1/4 teaspoon cayenne pepper, or more to taste
- 3/4 teaspoon dried oregano
- 1 1/2 pounds large shrimp, peeled and deveined
- 1/4 teaspoon garlic powder
- 1 tablespoon vegetable oil
- 1/4 teaspoon salt

DIRECTIONS

1. Combine paprika, thyme, oregano, garlic powder, salt, pepper, and cayenne pepper in a sealable plastic bag; shake to mix. Add shrimp and shake to coat.
2. Heat oil in a large non-stick skillet over medium high heat. Cook and stir shrimp in hot oil until they are bright pink on the outside and the meat is no longer transparent in the center, about 4 minutes.

MANDI'S CHEESY POTATO SOUP

Servings: 5 | Prep: 10m | Cooks: 35m | Total: 45m

NUTRITION FACTS

Calories: 466 | Carbohydrates: 51g | Fat: 21.5g | Protein: 18.7g | Cholesterol: 45mg

INGREDIENTS

- 5 potatoes, peeled and cubed
- 3 tablespoons margarine, melted
- 1 small carrot, finely chopped
- 3 tablespoons all-purpose flour
- 1/2 stalk celery, finely chopped
- 1 1/2 teaspoons steak seasoning
- 1 1/2 cups water
- 1 teaspoon ground black pepper
- 1 teaspoon salt
- 2 cups shredded four-cheese blend
- 2 1/2 cups milk

DIRECTIONS

1. In a large pot over medium heat, combine potatoes, carrot, celery, water and salt. Bring to a boil, then reduce heat, cover and simmer until potatoes are tender, 15 to 20 minutes. Once tender, stir in milk.
2. In a small bowl, combine melted margarine, flour, steak seasoning and pepper. Stir into soup, increase heat to medium, and cook, stirring, until thick and bubbly. Remove from heat and stir in cheese until melted. Let stand 5 to 10 minutes before serving.

THAI SPICY BASIL CHICKEN FRIED RICE

Servings: 6 | Prep: 30m | Cooks: 10m | Total: 40m

NUTRITION FACTS

Calories: 794 | Carbohydrates: 116.4g | Fat: 22.1g | Protein: 29.1g | Cholesterol: 46mg

INGREDIENTS

- 3 tablespoons oyster sauce
- 1 pound boneless, skinless chicken breast, cut into thin strips
- 2 tablespoons fish sauce
- 1 red pepper, seeded and thinly sliced
- 1 teaspoon white sugar

- 1 onion, thinly sliced
- 1/2 cup peanut oil for frying
- 2 cups sweet Thai basil
- 4 cups cooked jasmine rice, chilled
- 1 cucumber, sliced (optional)
- 6 large cloves garlic clove, crushed
- 1/2 cup cilantro sprigs (optional)
- 2 serrano peppers, crushed

DIRECTIONS

1. Whisk together the oyster sauce, fish sauce, and sugar in a bowl.
2. Heat the oil in a wok over medium-high heat until the oil begins to smoke. Add the garlic and serrano peppers, stirring quickly. Stir in the chicken, bell pepper, onion and oyster sauce mixture; cook until the chicken is no longer pink. Raise heat to high and stir in the chilled rice; stir quickly until the sauce is blended with the rice. Use the back of a spoon to break up any rice sticking together.
3. Remove from heat and mix in the basil leaves. Garnish with sliced cucumber and cilantro as desired.

CABBAGE AND SMOKED SAUSAGE PASTA

Servings: 6 | Prep: 15m | Cooks: 20m | Total: 35m

NUTRITION FACTS

Calories: 845 | Carbohydrates: 68.5g | Fat: 51.2g | Protein: 30.9g | Cholesterol: 95mg

INGREDIENTS

- 1 (16 ounce) package farfalle (bow tie) pasta
- 1 large head green cabbage, shredded
- 1/2 cup butter
- salt and pepper to taste
- 2 cloves garlic, minced
- 1 pound smoked sausage, sliced
- 1/4 cup olive oil
- 1/4 cup grated Parmesan cheese

DIRECTIONS

1. Fill a large pot with lightly salted water and bring to a rolling boil over high heat. Once the water is boiling, stir in the bow tie pasta and return to a boil. Cook the pasta uncovered, stirring occasionally,

until the pasta has cooked through, but is still firm to the bite, about 12 minutes. Drain well in a colander set in the sink.
2. Melt the butter in a large pot over medium heat. Add the garlic, olive oil, and cabbage; season with salt and pepper; cook until tender, about 15 minutes. Stir in the sausage and bow tie pasta; cook until completely heated, about 5 minutes more. Top with Parmesan cheese and serve immediately.

CARAMELIZED BUTTERNUT SQUASH SOUP

Servings: 12 | Prep: 20m | Cooks: 30m | Total: 50m

NUTRITION FACTS

Calories: 189 | Carbohydrates: 24.9g | Fat: 10.3g | Protein: 2.9g | Cholesterol: 23mg

INGREDIENTS

- 3 tablespoons extra-virgin olive oil
- 4 cups chicken broth, or more as needed
- 3 pounds butternut squash, peeled and cubed
- 1/4 cup honey
- 1 large onion, sliced
- 1/2 cup heavy whipping cream
- 3 tablespoons butter
- 1 pinch ground nutmeg, or more to taste
- 1 tablespoon sea salt
- salt to taste
- 1 teaspoon freshly-cracked white pepper
- ground white pepper to taste

DIRECTIONS

1. Heat olive oil in a large pot over high heat. Cook and stir squash in hot oil until completely browned, about 10 minutes. Stir onion, butter, sea salt, and cracked white pepper into the squash; cook and stir together until the onions are completely tender and beginning to brown, about 10 minutes.
2. Pour chicken broth and honey over the mixture; bring to a boil, reduce heat to medium-low, and cook at a simmer until the squash is tender, about 5 minutes.
3. Pour the mixture into a blender no more than half full. Cover and hold lid in place; pulse a few times before leaving on to blend. Puree in batches until smooth.
4. Stir cream, nutmeg, salt, and ground white pepper into the soup to serve.

ROASTED TOMATO SOUP

Servings: 6 | Prep: 10m | Cooks: 50m | Total: 1h

NUTRITION FACTS

Calories: 140 | Carbohydrates: 14.7g | Fat: 7.6g | Protein: 5.4g | Cholesterol: 3mg

INGREDIENTS

- 3 pounds roma (plum) tomatoes, quartered
- 1 1/2 teaspoons freshly ground black pepper
- 1 yellow onion, halved and quartered
- 3 cloves garlic, halved
- 1/2 red bell pepper, chopped
- 5 cups low-sodium chicken broth
- 3 tablespoons olive oil
- 2 teaspoons dried basil
- 1 tablespoon sea salt
- 1 teaspoon dried parsley

DIRECTIONS

1. Preheat oven to 400 degrees F (200 degrees C). Line a large baking sheet with aluminum foil.
2. Spread tomatoes, onion, and red bell pepper in 1 layer onto the prepared baking sheet. Drizzle olive oil over tomato mixture and season with salt and pepper.
3. Roast in the preheated oven for 30 minutes; add garlic and continue roasting until tomato mixture is tender, about 15 more minutes.
4. Bring chicken broth, basil, and parsley to a boil in a large stockpot; reduce heat and simmer.
5. Put half the tomato mixture into a blender. Cover and hold lid down; pulse a few times before leaving on to blend until smooth, adding a small amount of the warm chicken broth if liquid is needed. Pour pureed tomato mixture into stockpot with chicken broth. Puree remaining half of tomato mixture and add to chicken stock mixture, mixing well. Simmer for 5 minutes.

CALIFORNIA MELT

Servings: 4 | Prep: 15m | Cooks: 2m | Total: 17m

NUTRITION FACTS

Calories: 335 | Carbohydrates: 21.1g | Fat: 22.5g | Protein: 15.6g | Cholesterol: 26mg

INGREDIENTS

- 4 slices whole-grain bread, lightly toasted
- 1/3 cup sliced toasted almonds
- 1 avocado, sliced
- 1 tomato, sliced
- 1 cup sliced mushrooms
- 4 slices Swiss cheese

DIRECTIONS

1. Preheat the oven broiler.
2. Lay the toasted bread out on a baking sheet. Top each slice of bread with 1/4 of the avocado, mushrooms, almonds, and tomato slices. Top each with a slice of Swiss cheese.
3. Broil the open-face sandwiches until the cheese melts and begins to bubble, about 2 minutes. Serve the sandwiches warm.

QUICK AND SUPER EASY CHICKEN AND DUMPLINGS
Servings: 6 | Prep: 5m | Cooks: 15m | Total: 20m

NUTRITION FACTS

Calories: 361 | Carbohydrates: 29.6g | Fat: 15.1g | Protein: 25g | Cholesterol: 63mg

INGREDIENTS

- 2 1/4 cups biscuit baking mix
- 2 (14 ounce) cans chicken broth
- 2/3 cup milk
- 2 (10 ounce) cans chunk chicken, drained

DIRECTIONS

1. In a medium bowl, stir together the biscuit mix and milk just until it pulls together. Set aside.
2. Pour the cans of chicken broth into a saucepan along with the chicken; bring to a boil. Once the broth is at a steady boil, take a handful of biscuit dough and flatten it in your hand. Tear off 1 to 2 inch pieces and drop them into the boiling broth. Make sure they are fully immersed at least for a moment. Once all of the dough is in the pot, carefully stir so that the newest dough clumps get covered by the broth. Cover, and simmer over medium heat for about 10 minutes, stirring occasionally.

VEGAN BLACK BEAN BURGERS
Servings: 4 | Prep: 15m | Cooks: 20m | Total: 35m

NUTRITION FACTS

Calories: 264 | Carbohydrates: 51.7g | Fat: 1.4g | Protein: 11.6g | Cholesterol: 0mg

INGREDIENTS

- 1 (15 ounce) can black beans, drained and rinsed
- 1 teaspoon chili powder

- 1/3 cup chopped sweet onion
- 1 teaspoon ground cumin
- 1 tablespoon minced garlic
- 1 teaspoon seafood seasoning (such as Old Bay)
- 3 baby carrots, grated (optional)
- 1/4 teaspoon salt
- 1/4 cup minced green bell pepper (optional)
- 1/4 teaspoon ground black pepper
- 1 tablespoon cornstarch
- 2 slices whole-wheat bread, torn into small crumbs
- 1 tablespoon warm water
- 3/4 cup unbleached flour, or as needed
- 3 tablespoons chile-garlic sauce (such as Sriracha), or to taste

DIRECTIONS

1. Preheat oven to 350 degrees F (175 degrees C). Grease a baking sheet.
2. Mash black beans in a bowl; add onion, garlic, carrots, and green bell pepper. Mix.
3. Whisk cornstarch, water, chile-garlic sauce, chili powder, cumin, seafood seasoning, salt, and black pepper together in a separate small bowl. Stir cornstarch mixture into black bean mixture.
4. Mix whole-wheat bread into bean mixture. Stir flour, 1/4 cup at a time, into bean mixture until a sticky batter forms.
5. Spoon 'burger-sized' mounds of batter onto the prepared baking sheet, about a 3/4-inch thickness per mound. Shape into burgers.
6. Bake in the preheated oven until cooked in the center and crisp in the outside, about 10 minutes on each side.

SHRIMP AND PASTA SHELL SALAD

Servings: 8 | Prep: 25m | Cooks: 10m | Total: 2h35m

NUTRITION FACTS

Calories: 451 | Carbohydrates: 33.8g | Fat: 28.8g | Protein: 15.4g | Cholesterol: 99mg

INGREDIENTS

- 1 1/4 cups mayonnaise, or more if needed
- 1 (12 ounce) package small pasta shells
- 2 teaspoons Dijon mustard
- 1 pound cooked, peeled, and deveined small shrimp - cut in half
- 2 teaspoons ketchup
- 1/2 cup finely diced red bell pepper
- 1/4 teaspoon Worcestershire sauce
- 3/4 cup diced celery

- 1 teaspoon salt, or to taste
- salt and ground black pepper to taste
- 1 pinch cayenne pepper, or to taste
- 1 pinch paprika, for garnish
- 1 lemon, juiced
- 3 sprigs fresh dill, or as desired
- 1/3 cup chopped fresh dill

DIRECTIONS

1. Whisk 1 1/4 cup mayonnaise, Dijon mustard, ketchup, Worcestershire sauce, salt, and cayenne pepper together in a bowl; add lemon juice and 1/3 cup chopped dill. Whisk until thoroughly combined. Refrigerate.
2. Bring a pot of well-salted water to a boil and stir in pasta shells; cook until tender, 8 to 10 minutes. Drain and rinse with cold water to cool pasta slightly; drain again. Transfer to a large bowl.
3. Toss shrimp with pasta; add red bell pepper, celery, and dressing to pasta and shrimp. Mix thoroughly to coat and fill shells with dressing. Cover bowl with plastic wrap and refrigerate until chilled, 2 to 3 hours.
4. Stir salad again before serving and season to taste with more salt, black pepper, lemon juice, and cayenne pepper if desired. If salad seems a little dry, mix in a little more mayonnaise. Garnish with paprika and sprigs of dill.

HAM AND BEANS AND MORE

Servings: 8 | Prep: 30m | Cooks: 6h | Total: 14h30m | Additional: 8h

NUTRITION FACTS

Calories: 459 | Carbohydrates: 39.9g | Fat: 22.3g | Protein: 25.5g | Cholesterol: 47mg

INGREDIENTS

- 1 pound dried Great Northern beans, sorted and rinsed
- 1 tablespoon butter
- 4 cups water
- 1 tablespoon olive oil
- 1/4 cup celery, chopped
- 2 leeks (bulb only), cut in half lengthwise
- 1 small onion, chopped
- 1 pound cooked ham, cut into bite-size pieces
- 2 bay leaves
- 5 slices bacon
- 1/4 teaspoon ground cumin
- 4 cups chicken stock
- 1/2 teaspoon garlic powder

- 1 pinch sea salt to taste
- 1 teaspoon dried parsley
- 1 pinch fresh ground black pepper to taste

DIRECTIONS

1. Place the beans into a large container and cover with several inches of cool water; let stand 8 hours to overnight. Drain and rinse before using.
2. Combine the soaked beans, 4 cups of water, celery, onion, bay leaves, cumin, garlic powder, and parsley into a slow cooker.
3. Melt the butter with the olive oil in a skillet over medium heat; cook and stir the leeks in the butter mixture until tender and the smaller pieces start to brown, 8 to 10 minutes. Transfer the leeks to the slow cooker. In the same pan, cook and stir the ham until the edges start to brown; stir into the soup. Place the bacon into the hot skillet, and pan-fry until the bacon is crisp, about 10 minutes. Cut the bacon into bite-size pieces and stir into the soup. Pour the chicken stock into the hot skillet, and stir to dissolve any brown flavor bits from the skillet; pour the chicken stock into the soup. Season with sea salt and pepper.
4. Set the cooker to Low cook the soup until the beans are very tender, 6 to 8 hours. Roughly mash about half the beans with a potato masher to thicken the soup.

PESTO PASTA CAPRESE SALAD

Servings: 6 | Prep: 10m | Cooks: 10m | Total: 20m

NUTRITION FACTS

Calories: 169 | Carbohydrates: 17.1g | Fat: 8.3g | Protein: 6.1g | Cholesterol: 10mg

INGREDIENTS

- 1 1/2 cups rotini pasta
- 1/8 teaspoon ground black pepper
- 3 tablespoons pesto, or to taste
- 1/2 cup halved grape tomatoes
- 1 tablespoon extra-virgin olive oil
- 1/2 cup small (pearlini) fresh mozzarella balls
- 1/4 teaspoon salt, or to taste
- 2 leaves fresh basil leaves, finely shredded
- 1/4 teaspoon granulated garlic

DIRECTIONS

1. Bring a large pot of lightly salted water to a boil; cook the rotini at a boil until tender yet firm to the bite, about 8 minutes; drain.
2. Mix pesto, olive oil, salt, granulated garlic, and black pepper in a bowl; add rotini. Toss to coat. Fold in tomatoes, mozzarella, and fresh basil.

CAPRESE SALAD WITH BALSAMIC REDUCTION
Servings: 4 | Prep: 15m | Cooks: 10m | Total: 25m

NUTRITION FACTS

Calories: 580 | Carbohydrates: 34.8g | Fat: 38.8g | Protein: 22g | Cholesterol: 89mg

INGREDIENTS

- 1 cup balsamic vinegar
- 1/4 teaspoon salt
- 1/4 cup honey
- 1/4 teaspoon ground black pepper
- 3 large tomatoes, cut into 1/2-inch slices
- 1/2 cup fresh basil leaves
- 1 (16 ounce) package fresh mozzarella cheese, cut into 1/4-inch slices
- 1/4 cup extra-virgin olive oil

DIRECTIONS

1. Stir balsamic vinegar and honey together in a small saucepan and place over high heat. Bring to a boil, reduce heat to low, and simmer until the vinegar mixture has reduced to 1/3 cup, about 10 minutes. Set the balsamic reduction aside to cool.
2. Arrange alternate slices of tomato and mozzarella cheese decoratively on a serving platter. Sprinkle with salt and black pepper, spread fresh basil leaves over the salad, and drizzle with olive oil and the balsamic reduction.

CLASSIC CUBAN MIDNIGHT (MEDIANOCHE) SANDWICH
Servings: 4 | Prep: 15m | Cooks: 8m | Total: 23m

NUTRITION FACTS

Calories: 1453 | Carbohydrates: 69.1g | Fat: 88.4g | Protein: 92.1g | Cholesterol: 275mg

INGREDIENTS

- 4 sweet bread rolls

- 1 pound thinly sliced fully cooked pork
- 1/2 cup mayonnaise
- 1 pound sliced Swiss cheese
- 1/4 cup prepared mustard
- 1 cup dill pickle slices
- 1 pound thinly sliced cooked ham
- 2 tablespoons butter, melted

DIRECTIONS

1. Split the sandwich rolls in half, and spread mustard and mayonnaise liberally onto the cut sides. On each sandwich, place and equal amount of Swiss cheese, ham and pork in exactly that order. Place a few pickles onto each one, and put the top of the roll onto the sandwich. Brush the tops with melted butter.
2. Press each sandwich in a sandwich press heated to medium-high heat. If a sandwich press is not available, use a large skillet over medium-high heat, and press the sandwiches down using a sturdy plate or skillet. Some indoor grills may be good for this also. Cook for 5 to 8 minutes, keeping sandwiches pressed. If using a skillet, you may want to flip them once for even browning. Slice diagonally and serve hot.

EASY CLOUD BREAD

Servings: 5 | Prep: 10m | Cooks: 30m | Total: 40m

NUTRITION FACTS

Calories: 93 | Carbohydrates: 3.1g | Fat: 6.9g | Protein: 4.6g | Cholesterol: 124mg

INGREDIENTS

- 3 large eggs, separated
- 2 ounces cream cheese, very soft
- 1/4 teaspoon cream of tartar
- 1 tablespoon white sugar

DIRECTIONS

1. Preheat oven to 350 degrees F (175 degrees C). Line a baking sheet with parchment paper.
2. Beat egg whites and cream of tartar together in a bowl until stiff peaks form.
3. Mix egg yolks, cream cheese, and sugar together in a separate bowl using a wooden spoon and then mixing with a hand-held egg beater until mixture is very smooth and has no visible cream cheese. Gently fold egg whites into cream cheese mixture, taking care not to deflate the egg whites.

4. Carefully scoop mixture onto the prepared baking sheet, forming 5 to 6 "buns".
5. Bake in the preheated oven until cloud bread is lightly browned, about 30 minutes.

CREAMY TOMATO-BASIL SOUP

Servings: 8 | Prep: 10m | Cooks: 45m | Total: 55m

NUTRITION FACTS

Calories: 258 | Carbohydrates: 10.7g | Fat: 23.9g | Protein: 2.8g | Cholesterol: 56mg

INGREDIENTS

- 1/4 cup butter
- salt to taste
- 1/4 cup olive oil
- ground black pepper to taste
- 1 1/2 cups chopped onions
- 1 quart chicken broth
- 3 pounds tomatoes - cored, peeled, and quartered
- 1 cup heavy cream
- 1/2 cup chopped fresh basil leaves
- 8 sprigs fresh basil for garnish

DIRECTIONS

5. Heat the butter and olive oil in a large pot over medium heat. Stir in onions and cook until tender. Mix in tomatoes and chopped basil. Season with salt and pepper. Pour in the chicken broth, reduce heat to low, and continue cooking 15 minutes.
6. Transfer soup to a blender (or use an immersible hand blender), and blend until smooth. Return to the pot, and bring to a boil. Reduce heat to low, and gradually mix in the heavy cream. Pour soup through a strainer before serving. Garnish each serving with a sprig of basil.

VIETNAMESE SANDWICH

Servings: 4 | Prep: 10m | Cooks: 5m | Total: 15m

NUTRITION FACTS

Calories: 627 | Carbohydrates: 72.1g | Fat: 12.1g | Protein: 55.3g | Cholesterol: 124mg

INGREDIENTS

- 4 boneless pork loin chops, cut 1/4 inch thick
- 1 small red onion, sliced into rings
- 4 (7 inch) French bread baguettes, split lengthwise

- 1 medium cucumber, peeled and sliced lengthwise
- 4 teaspoons mayonnaise, or to taste
- 2 tablespoons chopped fresh cilantro
- 1 ounce chile sauce with garlic
- 1 small red onion, sliced into rings
- 1/4 cup fresh lime juice

DIRECTIONS

1. Preheat the oven's broiler. Place the pork chops on a broiling pan and set under the broiler. Cook for about 5 minutes, turning once, or until browned on each side.
2. Open the French rolls and spread mayonnaise on the insides. Place one of the cooked pork chops into each roll. Spread chile sauce directly on the meat. Sprinkle with a little lime juice and top with slices of onion, cucumber, cilantro, salt and pepper. Finish with another quick drizzle of lime juice.

STEF'S SUPER CHEESY GARLIC BREAD

Servings: 8 | Prep: 10m | Cooks: 10m | Total: 20m

NUTRITION FACTS

Calories: 555 | Carbohydrates: 35.4g | Fat: 39g | Protein: 17.5g | Cholesterol: 68mg

INGREDIENTS

- 1/2 cup butter, softened
- 1 1/4 cups Parmesan cheese
- 3/4 cup mayonnaise
- 1 1/2 cups shredded Monterey Jack cheese
- 1 bunch green onions, chopped
- 1 (1 pound) loaf French bread, halved lengthwise
- 3 cloves garlic, minced

DIRECTIONS

1. Preheat an oven to 350 degrees F (175 degrees C).
2. Combine the butter, mayonnaise, green onions, garlic, Parmesan cheese, and Monterey Jack cheese in a large bowl. Cut each half of French bread into 4 pieces. Spread the cheese mixture evenly on the bread pieces.
3. Bake in the preheated oven for 8 minutes. Set the oven to broil; broil until hot and bubbly, about 2 additional minutes.

HEARTY CHICKEN AND RICE SOUP

Servings: 8 | Prep: 20m | Cooks: 25m | Total: 45m

NUTRITION FACTS

Calories: 167 | Carbohydrates: 18.3g | Fat: 2.8g | Protein: 16.1g | Cholesterol: 22mg

INGREDIENTS

- 10 cups chicken broth
- 1/2 teaspoon dried thyme leaves
- 1 onion, chopped
- 1 bay leaf
- 1 cup sliced celery
- 3/4 pound chicken, cut into cubes
- 1 cup sliced carrots
- 2 cups cooked rice
- 1/4 cup snipped parsley
- 2 tablespoons lime juice
- 1/2 teaspoon cracked black pepper
- lime for garnish

DIRECTIONS

1. Combine chicken broth, onion, celery, carrots, parsley, pepper, thyme, and bay leaf in a Dutch oven; bring to a boil. Reduce heat to low; simmer until the onion and celery begin to soften, 10 to 15 minutes. Stir chicken into the simmering broth; cook until the chicken is no longer pink in the middle, 5 to 10 minutes. Remove and discard bay leaf. Stir rice and lime juice into the broth; cook and stir just until rice is hot and grains separate, about 1 minute. Garnish with lime slices.

TORTELLINI, STEAK, AND CAESAR

Servings: 4 | Prep: 15m | Cooks: 15m | Total: 30m

NUTRITION FACTS

Calories: 671 | Carbohydrates: 46.6g | Fat: 42.1g | Protein: 27.8g | Cholesterol: 83mg

INGREDIENTS

- 1 (9 ounce) package cheese tortellini
- 2 heads romaine lettuce, torn into bite-size pieces
- 1 pound flank steak
- 2 (2.25 ounce) cans small pitted black olives, drained

- garlic powder to taste
- 1 cup Caesar-style croutons
- salt and pepper to taste
- 2 small fresh tomatoes, chopped
- 1 tablespoon olive oil
- 1 (8 ounce) bottle Caesar salad dressing

DIRECTIONS

1. Bring a large pot of lightly salted water to a boil. Place pasta in the pot, cook for 7 to 9 minutes, until al dente, and drain.
2. Preheat the oven broiler. Season steak with garlic powder, salt, and pepper; rub with olive oil. Place steak in a baking dish, and broil 5 minutes on each side, or to desired doneness. Slice diagonally into thin strips.
3. In a bowl, toss the cooked tortellini, lettuce, olives, croutons, tomatoes, and dressing. Top with steak strips to serve.

HEARTY CHICKEN AND RICE SOUP

Servings: 8 | Prep: 20m | Cooks: 25m | Total: 45m

NUTRITION FACTS

Calories: 167 | Carbohydrates: 18.3g | Fat: 2.8g | Protein: 16.1g | Cholesterol: 22mg

INGREDIENTS

- 10 cups chicken broth
- 1/2 teaspoon dried thyme leaves
- 1 onion, chopped
- 1 bay leaf
- 1 cup sliced celery
- 3/4 pound chicken, cut into cubes
- 1 cup sliced carrots
- 2 cups cooked rice
- 1/4 cup snipped parsley
- 2 tablespoons lime juice
- 1/2 teaspoon cracked black pepper
- lime for garnish

DIRECTIONS

1. Combine chicken broth, onion, celery, carrots, parsley, pepper, thyme, and bay leaf in a Dutch oven; bring to a boil. Reduce heat to low; simmer until the onion and celery begin to soften, 10 to 15 minutes. Stir chicken into the simmering broth; cook until the chicken is no longer pink in the middle, 5 to 10 minutes. Remove and discard bay leaf. Stir rice and lime juice into the broth; cook and stir just until rice is hot and grains separate, about 1 minute. Garnish with lime slices.

MIMI'S ZUCCHINI PIE
Servings: 8 | Prep: 25m | Cooks: 35m | Total: 1h

NUTRITION FACTS

Calories: 182 | Carbohydrates: 12.6g | Fat: 12.4g | Protein: 6g | Cholesterol: 95mg

INGREDIENTS

- 4 eggs
- 1 1/2 cups sliced zucchini
- 1/4 cup vegetable oil
- 1 1/2 cups sliced yellow squash
- salt and pepper to taste
- 1/4 cup chopped onion
- 1 teaspoon baking powder
- 1 large ripe tomato, sliced
- 1 cup all-purpose baking mix
- 1/4 cup grated Parmesan cheese

DIRECTIONS

1. Preheat oven to 350 degrees F (175 degrees C). Lightly grease a 9 inch deep dish pie plate.
2. Whisk together eggs and oil in a bowl with salt and pepper. Stir in baking powder and baking mix until moistened. Gently fold in zucchini, summer squash, and onion. Pour into prepared pie plate, and arrange sliced tomato over top. Sprinkle with Parmesan cheese to taste.
3. Bake in preheated oven until puffed and golden brown, about 35 minutes.

HALLOWEEN EYE OF NEWT
Servings: 12 | Prep: 10m | Cooks: 15m | Total: 25m

NUTRITION FACTS

Calories: 99 | Carbohydrates: 1.8g | Fat: 7.5g | Protein: 6.5g | Cholesterol: 186mg

INGREDIENTS

- 12 eggs
- 1 tablespoon prepared yellow mustard
- 1 tablespoon sweet pickle relish
- 2 drops green food coloring, or as needed
- 1 tablespoon mayonnaise
- 1 (6 ounce) can sliced black olives, drained
- 1 pinch celery salt

DIRECTIONS

1. Place all of the eggs into a large pot so they can rest on the bottom in a single layer. Fill with just enough cold water to cover the eggs. Bring to a boil, then cover, remove from the heat and let stand for about 15 minutes. Rinse under cold water or add some ice to the water and let the eggs cool completely. Peel and slice in half lengthwise.
2. Remove the yolks from the eggs and place them in a bowl. Mix in the relish, mayonnaise, celery salt, mustard, and food coloring. Spoon this filling into the egg whites and place them on a serving tray. Round the top of the filling using the spoon. Place an olive slice on each yolk to create the center of the eye. Dab a tiny bit of mayonnaise in the center of the olive as a finishing touch.

TURKEY SLOPPY JOES

Servings: 8 | Prep: 15m | Cooks: 15m | Total: 30m

NUTRITION FACTS

Calories: 393 | Carbohydrates: 36.4g | Fat: 13.3g | Protein: 32.8g | Cholesterol: 105mg

INGREDIENTS

- 2 1/2 pounds ground turkey
- 2 tablespoons prepared yellow mustard
- 1/2 cup chopped onion
- 1 tablespoon vinegar
- 1/2 cup chopped green bell pepper
- 1/2 teaspoon celery seed
- 1/2 cup chopped tomato
- 1/2 teaspoon ground black pepper
- 1 cup no-salt-added ketchup
- 1/2 teaspoon red pepper flakes, or to taste
- 7 tablespoons barbeque sauce
- 8 hamburger bun, split and toasted

DIRECTIONS

1. Heat a nonstick skillet over medium heat; cook and stir turkey, onion, bell pepper, and tomato until turkey is crumbly and no longer pink, about 5 minutes. Stir in ketchup, barbeque sauce, mustard, vinegar, celery seed, black pepper, and red pepper flakes. Reduce heat to low and simmer for 10 minutes, stirring occasionally. Serve turkey mixture on toasted hamburger buns.

VEGAN BROCCOLI SOUP

Servings: 4 | Prep: 15m | Cooks: 20m | Total: 35m

NUTRITION FACTS

Calories: 353.4 | Carbohydrates: 44.6g | Protein: 12.8g | Cholesterol: 0mg

INGREDIENTS

- 1 cup raw cashews
- 4 1/2 cups coarsely chopped broccoli
- 5 cups vegetable broth, divided
- 1 teaspoon dried basil
- 2 medium (2-1/4" to 3" dia, raw)s Yukon Gold potatoes, cut into 1/2-inch cubes
- 1 teaspoon fine sea salt
- 1 onion, finely chopped
- 1/4 teaspoon freshly ground black pepper

DIRECTIONS

1. Blend cashews and 1 cup vegetable broth in a blender until smooth, about 1 minute.
2. Pour the remaining 4 cups vegetable broth into a large pot; add potatoes and onion. Bring to a simmer, cover, and cook for 5 minutes. Stir in broccoli and basil; return to a simmer. Cover and cook until potatoes are tender, about 10 minutes.
3. Stir cashew mixture into soup; add salt and black pepper. Bring to a simmer and immediately remove from heat. Transfer about half the soup to a blender; blend until smooth. Return blended soup to pot and stir well. Serve immediately.

REUBEN SANDWICH

Servings: 4 | Prep: 15m | Cooks: 10m | Total: 25m

NUTRITION FACTS

Calories: 793 | Carbohydrates: 50.2g | Fat: 51.7g | Protein: 34.2g | Cholesterol: 107mg

INGREDIENTS

- 8 slices rye bread
- 8 slices Swiss cheese
- 3/4 cup thousand island dressing
- 8 slices pastrami
- 1 (16 ounce) can sauerkraut, drained
- 1/4 cup margarine, softened

DIRECTIONS

1. Spread each slice of bread with thousand island dressing. Top 4 of the bread slices with sauerkraut, cheese and pastrami. Place remaining bread slices on sandwich. Spread margarine on the outsides of each sandwich.
2. Heat a large skillet over medium high heat. Grill until browned, then turn and grill until heated through, and cheese is melted.

HAWAIIAN HAM AND CHEESE SLIDERS
Servings: 12 | Prep: 15m | Cooks: 35m | Total: 50m

NUTRITION FACTS

Calories: 484 | Carbohydrates: 46.5g | Fat: 16.5g | Protein: 25.7g | Cholesterol: 99mg

INGREDIENTS

- cooking spray (such as Crisco)
- 2 teaspoons Worcestershire sauce, or more to taste
- 1/2 cup butter
- 1 (12 count) package Hawaiian sweet rolls, split, or more as needed
- 1 onion, minced
- 1 pound sliced deli ham, or more as needed
- 3 tablespoons Dijon mustard
- 8 slices Swiss cheese, or more as needed
- 1 tablespoon poppy seeds

DIRECTIONS

1. Preheat oven to 350 degrees F (175 degrees C). Spray a 9x13-inch baking dish with cooking spray.
2. Melt butter in a saucepan over medium-low heat; cook and stir onion until softened, 5 to 10 minutes. Add mustard, poppy seeds, and Worcestershire sauce; cook and stir for 5 minutes.
3. Arrange the bottoms from each roll in the prepared baking dish. Spoon 2/3 the onion mixture over the roll bottoms. Add ham and Swiss cheese to each roll. Put tops of rolls over the Swiss cheese layer. Brush the remaining 1/3 onion mixture over tops of rolls. Cover dish with aluminum foil.

4. Bake in the preheated oven for 15 minutes. Remove aluminum foil and bake until tops of rolls are lightly browned, 5 to 10 minutes.

SPINACH AND BACON QUICHE

Servings: 8 | Prep: 15m | Cooks: 35m | Total: 50m

NUTRITION FACTS

Calories: 506 | Carbohydrates: 14.3g | Fat: 41.5g | Protein: 19.8g | Cholesterol: 240mg

INGREDIENTS

- 3/4 pound sliced bacon
- 5 dashes hot pepper sauce, or to taste
- 1 (9 inch) single refrigerated pie crust
- 1 (10 ounce) package frozen chopped spinach - thawed, drained and squeezed dry
- 6 eggs, beaten
- 1 1/2 cups shredded Cheddar cheese
- 1 1/2 cups heavy cream
- 1/2 cup chopped green onion
- salt and ground black pepper to taste
- 1/4 cup grated Parmesan cheese
- 2 dashes Worcestershire sauce

DIRECTIONS

1. Preheat oven to 375 degrees F (190 degrees C).
2. Place the bacon in a large, deep skillet, and cook over medium-high heat, turning occasionally, until evenly browned, about 10 minutes. Drain the bacon slices on a paper towel-lined plate. Chop when cool.
3. Fit the pie crust into a 9-inch pie dish, and set aside.
4. In a bowl, whisk together the eggs, cream, salt, black pepper, Worcestershire sauce, and hot pepper sauce. Spread the spinach into the bottom of the pie crust; top with bacon, Cheddar cheese, and green onion. Pour the egg mixture over the filling, and sprinkle the quiche with Parmesan cheese.
5. Bake in the preheated oven until the top is lightly puffed and browned, and a knife inserted into the center of the quiche comes out clean, 35 to 45 minutes.

TRADITIONAL CREAMY COLESLAW

Servings: 12 | Prep: 10m | Cooks: 1h | Total: 1h10m

NUTRITION FACTS

Calories: 204 | Carbohydrates: 13.9g | Fat: 16.3g | Protein: 1.1g | Cholesterol: 12mg

INGREDIENTS

- 1 cup mayonnaise
- 1/2 teaspoon dry mustard
- 1/4 cup white sugar
- 1/2 teaspoon celery salt
- 2 tablespoons seasoned rice wine vinegar
- 1/2 teaspoon salt
- 1 1/2 tablespoons lemon juice
- 1/2 teaspoon ground black pepper
- 1 tablespoon prepared horseradish
- 1 (28 ounce) package coleslaw mix
- 1/2 teaspoon onion powder

DIRECTIONS

1. Whisk mayonnaise, sugar, rice wine vinegar, lemon juice, horseradish, onion powder, dry mustard, celery salt, salt, and black pepper in a large mixing bowl, stirring to dissolve sugar. Fold coleslaw mix into dressing. Cover bowl and refrigerate 1 hour before serving.

CREAM OF ASPARAGUS AND MUSHROOM SOUP

Servings: 8 | Prep: 15m | Cooks: 40m | Total: 55m

NUTRITION FACTS

Calories: 171 | Carbohydrates: 12.7g | Fat: 11.8g | Protein: 5.2g | Cholesterol: 29mg

INGREDIENTS

- 3 slices bacon
- 6 cups chicken broth
- 1 tablespoon bacon drippings
- 1 potato, peeled and diced
- 1/4 cup butter
- 1 pound fresh asparagus, tips set aside and stalks chopped
- 3 stalks celery, chopped
- salt and ground black pepper to taste
- 1 onion, diced
- 1 (8 ounce) package sliced fresh mushrooms
- 3 tablespoons all-purpose flour
- 3/4 cup half-and-half cream

DIRECTIONS

1. Place the bacon in a large, deep skillet, and cook over medium-high heat, turning occasionally, until evenly browned, about 10 minutes. Drain the bacon slices on a paper towel-lined plate. Crumble bacon when cool; set aside. Reserve 1 tablespoon of bacon drippings.
2. Melt butter with drippings in a saucepan over medium heat.
3. Cook and stir celery and onion in the saucepan until onion is translucent, about 4 minutes.
4. Whisk flour into the mixture and cook for 1 minute.
5. Whisk in chicken broth and bring to a boil.
6. Add potato and chopped asparagus stalks, reserving the asparagus tips for later. Season with salt and ground black pepper.
7. Reduce heat and simmer for 20 minutes.
8. Pour the soup into a blender, filling the pitcher no more than halfway full. Hold down the lid of the blender with a folded kitchen towel, and carefully start the blender, using a few quick pulses to get the soup moving before leaving it on to puree. Puree in batches until smooth and pour into a clean pot. Alternately, you can use a stick blender and puree the soup right in the cooking pot.
9. Cook and stir mushrooms and asparagus tips in the same skillet used for bacon until mushrooms give up their liquid, 5 to 8 minutes. Season with salt and ground black pepper, if needed.
10. Stir mushrooms, asparagus tips, and half-and-half cream to pureed soup. Cook until thoroughly heated.
11. Garnish soup with crumbled bacon.

HEARTY VEGAN SLOW-COOKER CHILI

Servings: 15 | Prep: 45m | Cooks: 5h10m | Total: 5h55m

NUTRITION FACTS

Calories: 134 | Carbohydrates: 24.8g | Fat: 2.4g | Protein: 6.3g | Cholesterol: 0mg

INGREDIENTS

- 1 tablespoon olive oil
- 1 tablespoon dried oregano
- 1 green bell pepper, chopped
- 1 tablespoon dried parsley
- 1 red bell pepper, chopped
- 1/2 teaspoon salt
- 1 yellow bell pepper, chopped
- 1/2 teaspoon ground black pepper
- 2 onions, chopped

- 2 (14.5 ounce) cans diced tomatoes with juice
- 4 cloves garlic, minced
- 1 (15 ounce) can black beans, rinsed and drained
- 1 (10 ounce) package frozen chopped spinach, thawed and drained
- 1 (15 ounce) can garbanzo beans, drained
- 1 cup frozen corn kernels, thawed
- 1 (15 ounce) can kidney beans, rinsed and drained
- 1 zucchini, chopped
- 2 (6 ounce) cans tomato paste
- 1 yellow squash, chopped
- 1 (8 ounce) can tomato sauce, or more if needed
- 6 tablespoons chili powder
- 1 cup vegetable broth, or more if needed
- 1 tablespoon ground cumin

DIRECTIONS

1. Heat olive oil in a large skillet over medium heat, and cook the green, red, and yellow bell peppers, onions, and garlic until the onions start to brown, 8 to 10 minutes. Place the mixture into a slow cooker. Stir in spinach, corn, zucchini, yellow squash, chili powder, cumin, oregano, parsley, salt, black pepper, tomatoes, black beans, garbanzo beans, kidney beans, and tomato paste until thoroughly mixed. Pour the tomato sauce and vegetable broth over the ingredients.
2. Set the cooker on Low, and cook until all vegetables are tender, 4 to 5 hours. Check seasoning; if chili is too thick, add more tomato sauce and vegetable broth to desired thickness. Cook an additional 1 to 2 hours to blend the flavors.

QUINOA VEGETABLE SALAD

Servings: 12 | Prep: 20m | Cooks: 25m | Total: 1h30m

NUTRITION FACTS

Calories: 148 | Carbohydrates: 22.9g | Fat: 4.5g | Protein: 4.6g | Cholesterol: 0mg

INGREDIENTS

- 1 teaspoon canola oil
- 1/2 cup diced cucumber
- 1 tablespoon minced garlic
- 1/2 cup frozen corn kernels, thawed
- 1/4 cup diced (yellow or purple) onion
- 1/4 cup diced red onion
- 2 1/2 cups water
- 1 1/2 tablespoons chopped fresh cilantro
- 2 teaspoons salt, or to taste

- 1 tablespoon chopped fresh mint
- 1/4 teaspoon ground black pepper
- 1 teaspoon salt
- 2 cups quinoa
- 1/4 teaspoon ground black pepper
- 3/4 cup diced fresh tomato
- 2 tablespoons olive oil
- 3/4 cup diced carrots
- 3 tablespoons balsamic vinegar
- 1/2 cup diced yellow bell pepper

DIRECTIONS

1. Heat the canola oil in a saucepan over medium heat. Cook and stir the garlic and 1/4 cup onion in the hot oil until the onion has softened and turned translucent, about 5 minutes. Pour in the water, 2 teaspoons salt, and 1/4 teaspoon black pepper and bring to a boil; stir the quinoa into the mixture, reduce heat to medium-low, and cover. Simmer until the quinoa is tender, about 20 minutes. Drain any remaining water from the quinoa with a mesh strainer and transfer to a large mixing bowl. Refrigerate until cold.
2. Stir the tomato, carrots, bell pepper, cucumber, corn, and 1/4 cup red onion into the chilled quinoa. Season with cilantro, mint, 1 teaspoon salt, and 1/4 teaspoon black pepper. Drizzle the olive oil and balsamic vinegar over the salad; gently stir until evenly mixed.

ITALIAN SUBS - RESTAURANT STYLE

Servings: 8 | Prep: 20m | Cooks: 1h | Total: 1h20m

NUTRITION FACTS

Calories: 708 | Carbohydrates: 40.4g | Fat: 47.3g | Protein: 29.2g | Cholesterol: 79mg

INGREDIENTS

- 1 head red leaf lettuce, rinsed and torn
- 1/4 teaspoon red pepper flakes
- 2 medium fresh tomatoes, chopped
- 1 pinch dried oregano
- 1 medium red onion, chopped
- 1/2 pound sliced Capacola sausage
- 6 tablespoons olive oil
- 1/2 pound thinly sliced Genoa salami
- 2 tablespoons white wine vinegar
- 1/4 pound thinly sliced prosciutto
- 2 tablespoons chopped fresh parsley
- 1/2 pound sliced provolone cheese

- 2 cloves garlic, chopped
- 4 submarine rolls, split
- 1 teaspoon dried basil
- 1 cup dill pickle slices

DIRECTIONS

1. In a large bowl, toss together the lettuce, tomatoes and onion. In a separate bowl, whisk together the olive oil, white wine vinegar, parsley, garlic, basil, red pepper flakes and oregano. Pour over the salad, and toss to coat evenly. Refrigerate for about 1 hour.
2. Spread the submarine rolls open, and layer the Capacola, salami, prosciutto, and provolone cheese evenly on each roll. Top with some of the salad, and as many pickle slices as desired. Close the rolls and serve.

JIM'S CHEDDAR ONION SODA BREAD

Servings: 12 | Prep: 15m | Cooks: 30m | Total: 55m

NUTRITION FACTS

Calories: 264 | Carbohydrates: 36.9g | Fat: 9.1g | Protein: 8.2g | Cholesterol: 24mg

INGREDIENTS

- 4 cups bread flour, plus more for dusting
- 1 1/4 cups buttermilk
- 1 1/2 teaspoons salt
- 2 tablespoons confectioners' sugar
- 1 tablespoon baking powder
- 3/4 cup finely chopped onion
- 6 tablespoons butter, softened
- 3/4 cup shredded Cheddar cheese

DIRECTIONS

1. Preheat oven to 425 degrees F (220 degrees C). Line a baking sheet with parchment paper.
2. In a large mixing bowl, whisk together bread flour, salt, and baking powder until thoroughly combined. Beat in the butter, buttermilk, and confectioners' sugar to make a dough; gently mix in the onion and Cheddar cheese. Divide dough in half, and shape each half into a ball. Place the loaves onto the prepared baking sheet, and gently flatten to about 2 inches thick. Dust each loaf with flour.
3. Bake on a preheated oven until browned, about 30 minutes. Cool on racks for a few minutes; serve warm.

CHILI RELLENO CASSEROLE

Servings: 8 | Prep: 10m | Cooks: 45m | Total: 55m

NUTRITION FACTS

Calories: 564 | Carbohydrates: 12.6g | Fat: 41.9g | Protein: 34.6g | Cholesterol: 211mg

INGREDIENTS

- 2 (7 ounce) cans whole green chiles, drained
- 1 1/2 (5 ounce) cans evaporated milk
- 1 pound shredded Cheddar cheese
- 1 pound shredded Monterey Jack cheese
- 4 eggs
- 2 (10 ounce) cans green enchilada sauce
- 2 tablespoons all-purpose flour

DIRECTIONS

1. Preheat oven to 400 degrees F (200 degrees C). Grease a 9x13-inch baking dish.
2. Split the chiles open, and spread half the chiles into the bottom of the prepared baking dish. Layer with the Cheddar cheese, and top with the rest of the canned chiles. Whisk together the eggs, flour, and evaporated milk in a bowl. Pour the mixture over the chiles and cheese.
3. Bake in the preheated oven until set, about 30 minutes; remove casserole, and top with the Monterey Jack cheese. Pour the green chili salsa over the top; return to oven, and bake until the cheese is melted, about 15 more minutes.

BLT

Servings: 1 | Prep: 5m | Cooks: 10m | Total: 15m

NUTRITION FACTS

Calories: 439 | Carbohydrates: 28.8g | Fat: 27.8g | Protein: 17.9g | Cholesterol: 45mg

INGREDIENTS

- 4 slices bacon
- 2 slices bread, toasted
- 2 leaves lettuce
- 1 tablespoon mayonnaise
- 2 slices tomato

DIRECTIONS

1. Cook the bacon in a large, deep skillet over medium-high heat until evenly browned, about 10 minutes. Drain the bacon slices on a paper towel-lined plate.
2. Arrange the cooked bacon, lettuce, and tomato slices on one slice of bread. Spread one side of remaining bread slice with the mayonnaise. Bring the two pieces together to make a sandwich.

SLOW COOKER GERMAN-STYLE PORK ROAST WITH SAUERKRAUT AND POTATOES

Servings: 8 | Prep: 20m | Cooks: 8h | Total: 8h20m

NUTRITION FACTS

Calories: 385 | Carbohydrates: 30.5g | Fat: 15.2g | Protein: 31.3g | Cholesterol: 83mg

INGREDIENTS

- 6 white potatoes, peeled and quartered
- 1 (3 pound) boneless pork loin roast
- 1 tablespoon minced garlic
- 1 (32 ounce) jar sauerkraut with liquid
- salt and pepper to taste
- 2 teaspoons caraway seeds

DIRECTIONS

1. Place the potatoes, garlic, salt, and pepper in a slow cooker; stir to coat. Season the pork roast with salt and pepper; lay atop the potatoes. Pour the sauerkraut over the roast; sprinkle with caraway seeds.
2. Cook in slow cooker on Low 8 to 10 hours.

SPICY GRILLED CHEESE SANDWICH

Servings: 2 | Prep: 2m | Cooks: 3m | Total: 5m

NUTRITION FACTS

Calories: 352 | Carbohydrates: 28.2g | Fat: 22.1g | Protein: 10.7g | Cholesterol: 57mg

INGREDIENTS

- 2 tablespoons butter or margarine
- 1 roma (plum) tomato, thinly sliced
- 4 slices white bread
- 1/4 small onion, chopped
- 2 slices American cheese
- 1 jalapeno pepper, chopped

DIRECTIONS

1. Heat a large skillet over low heat. Spread butter or margarine onto one side of two slices of bread. Place both pieces buttered side down in the skillet. Lay a slice of cheese on each one, and top with slices of tomato, onion and jalapeno. Butter one side of the remaining slices of bread, and place on top buttered side up. When the bottom of the sandwiches are toasted, flip and fry until brown on the other side.

SPENCE'S PESTO CHICKEN PASTA
Servings: 4 | Prep: 20m | Cooks: 25m | Total: 45m

NUTRITION FACTS

Calories: 512 | Carbohydrates: 53.5g | Fat: 23.3g | Protein: 26.1g | Cholesterol: 35mg

INGREDIENTS

- 1/2 pound linguine pasta
- 6 ounces roasted red peppers, drained and chopped
- 1 (8 ounce) skinless, boneless chicken breast, cut into small pieces
- 1 (7.5 ounce) jar marinated artichoke hearts, drained and quartered
- salt and ground black pepper to taste
- 3 ounces fresh spinach leaves
- 3 tablespoons olive oil
- 1/4 cup prepared basil pesto, or to taste
- 6 whole garlic cloves
- 1 tablespoon freshly grated Parmesan cheese, divided (optional)
- 4 ounces fresh mushrooms, halved

DIRECTIONS

1. Fill a large pot with lightly salted water and bring to a rolling boil over high heat. Once the water is boiling, stir in the linguine, and return to a boil. Cook the pasta uncovered, stirring occasionally, until the pasta has cooked through, but is still firm to the bite, about 11 minutes. Drain well in a colander set in the sink.
2. While the pasta is boiling, sprinkle the chicken with salt and black pepper. Heat the olive oil in a large skillet over medium heat, and cook the chicken pieces until lightly browned, about 10 minutes, stirring frequently. Stir in the garlic cloves, mushrooms, roasted red peppers, and artichoke hearts; reduce heat to a simmer, and cook until the mushrooms begin to give off their juices, 5 to 8 minutes. Stir in the spinach, and simmer just until the leaves are wilted, about 2 minutes.
3. Transfer the cooked linguine into a bowl, and toss with the basil pesto. Divide the pasta between 2 plates, and serve topped with the chicken mixture. Sprinkle Parmesan cheese over each plate to serve.

HARVEY HAM SANDWICHES

Servings: 24 | Prep: 30m | Cooks: 10h | Total: 10h30m

NUTRITION FACTS

Calories: 445 | Carbohydrates: 33.9g | Fat: 23.2g | Protein: 24.5g | Cholesterol: 65mg

INGREDIENTS

- 1 (6 pound) bone-in ham
- 1 pound brown sugar
- 1 (8 ounce) jar yellow mustard
- 24 dinner rolls, split

DIRECTIONS

1. Place the ham in a large pot or slow cooker, and fill with enough water to cover. Bring to a boil, then reduce the heat to low, and simmer for 8 to 10 hours. Remove the meat from the water, and allow to cool. If it has cooked long enough, it will fall into pieces as you pick it up.
2. Pull the ham apart into shreds once it is cool enough to handle. It doesn't have to be tiny shreds. Place the shredded ham into a slow cooker. Stir in the mustard and brown sugar, cover, and set to Low. Cook just until heated. Serve on dinner rolls. We don't use any other sandwich toppings with it, but that is a personal choice.

SPICY GRILLED CHEESE SANDWICH

Servings: 2 | Prep: 2m | Cooks: 3m | Total: 5m

NUTRITION FACTS

Calories: 352 | Carbohydrates: 28.2g | Fat: 22.1g | Protein: 10.7g | Cholesterol: 57mg

INGREDIENTS

- 2 tablespoons butter or margarine
- 1 roma (plum) tomato, thinly sliced
- 4 slices white bread
- 1/4 small onion, chopped
- 2 slices American cheese
- 1 jalapeno pepper, chopped

DIRECTIONS

1. Heat a large skillet over low heat. Spread butter or margarine onto one side of two slices of bread. Place both pieces buttered side down in the skillet. Lay a slice of cheese on each one, and top with slices of tomato, onion and jalapeno. Butter one side of the remaining slices of bread, and place on top buttered side up. When the bottom of the sandwiches are toasted, flip and fry until brown on the other side.

BEST GREEK QUINOA SALAD

Servings: 10 | Prep: 15m | Cooks: 15m | Total: 1h40m | Additional: 1h10m

NUTRITION FACTS

Calories: 227 | Carbohydrates: 25.8g | Fat: 10.6g | Protein: 7.4g | Cholesterol: 12mg

INGREDIENTS

- 3 1/2 cups chicken broth
- 4 ounces chopped feta cheese, or more to taste
- 2 cups quinoa
- 3 tablespoons olive oil
- 1 cup halved grape tomatoes
- 3 tablespoons red wine vinegar
- 3/4 cup chopped fresh parsley
- 2 cloves garlic, minced
- 1/2 cup sliced pitted kalamata olives
- 1 lemon, halved
- 1/2 cup minced red onion
- salt and ground black pepper to taste

DIRECTIONS

1. Bring broth and quinoa to a boil in a saucepan. Reduce heat to medium-low, cover, and simmer until quinoa is tender and water has been absorbed, 15 to 20 minutes. Transfer quinoa to a large bowl and set aside to cool, about 10 minutes.
2. Mix tomatoes, parsley, kalamata olives, onion, feta cheese, olive oil, vinegar, and garlic into quinoa. Squeeze lemon juice over quinoa salad, season with salt and pepper, and toss to coat. Chill in refrigerator, 1 to 4 hours.

MOTHER-IN-LAW EGGS

Servings: 12 | Prep: 15m | Cooks: 15m | Total: 30m

NUTRITION FACTS

Calories: 57 | Carbohydrates: 0.8g | Fat: 4.6g | Protein: 3.3g | Cholesterol: 93mg

INGREDIENTS

- 6 eggs
- 1 teaspoon white sugar
- 2 tablespoons mayonnaise
- salt and pepper to taste
- 1 tablespoon spicy brown mustard (such as Gulden's)
- paprika for garnish (optional)
- 1 teaspoon hot mustard (such as Sweet Hot Mister Mustard)
- 6 pimento-stuffed green olives, cut in half

DIRECTIONS

1. Place the eggs into a saucepan in a single layer and fill with water to cover the eggs by 1 inch. Cover the saucepan and bring the water to a boil over high heat. Remove from the heat and let the eggs stand in the hot water for 15 minutes. Drain. Cool the eggs under cold running water. Peel once cold. Halve the eggs lengthwise and scoop the yolks into a bowl. Mash the yolks with a fork.
2. Stir the mayonnaise, spicy brown mustard, hot mustard, sugar, salt, and pepper into the yolks until well combined. Spoon into a quart-size, resealable plastic bag. Snip a corner off the plastic bag.
3. Squeeze the yolk mixture into the egg halves, sprinkle each stuffed egg with paprika, and top with an olive half.

SHRIMP QUESADILLAS

Servings: 6 | Prep: 15m | Cooks: 1h | Total: 1h15m

NUTRITION FACTS

Calories: 246 | Carbohydrates: 18.5g | Fat: 16.4g | Protein: 6.7g | Cholesterol: 23mg

INGREDIENTS

- 1 sheet frozen puff pastry, thawed
- 1/3 cup seedless raspberry jam
- 1 (8 ounce) round Brie cheese
- 2 tablespoons chopped walnuts

DIRECTIONS

1. Preheat oven to 350 degrees F (175 degrees C). Line a baking sheet with aluminum foil and lightly grease with cooking spray.

2. Lay the puff pastry onto the prepared baking sheet. Center the Brie wheel onto the pastry. Spread the jam evenly over the top of the Brie. Sprinkle the walnuts atop the jam. Fold the puff pastry over the top of the Brie, sealing all openings.
3. Bake in preheated oven until the pastry is golden brown, about 20 minutes.

EMERGENCY GARLIC BREAD

Servings: 4 | Prep: 5m | Cooks: 4m | Total: 9m

NUTRITION FACTS

Calories: 160 | Carbohydrates: 22.3g | Fat: 5.9g | Protein: 4.4g | Cholesterol: 11mg

INGREDIENTS

- 4 hot dog buns
- 2 teaspoons garlic powder, or to taste
- 4 teaspoons butter, or as needed

DIRECTIONS

1. Preheat your oven's broiler, or a toaster oven.
2. Separate the bun halves, and spread butter onto the cut side of each one. Sprinkle some garlic powder over the butter.
3. Broil or toast until golden brown, about 4 minutes.

BLACK BEAN, CORN, AND TOMATO SALAD WITH FETA CHEESE

Servings: 12 | Prep: 1h | Cooks: 9h | Total: 10h | Additional: 8h

NUTRITION FACTS

Calories: 285 | Carbohydrates: 16.8g | Fat: 22.4g | Protein: 6.1g | Cholesterol: 17mg

INGREDIENTS

- 1 (14 ounce) can black beans, drained and rinsed
- 1 (8 ounce) package crumbled feta cheese
- 2 fresh tomatoes, chopped
- 1 clove garlic
- 1 large green bell pepper, chopped
- 1 pinch sea salt
- 1 cup fresh sweet white corn, cut from the cob

- 1/4 cup fresh lime juice
- 1 bunch green onions, sliced
- 1 teaspoon Dijon mustard
- 1 jicama, peeled and minced
- 1/4 teaspoon fresh-ground black pepper
- 1 (14 ounce) can black beans, drained and rinsed
- 1 cup olive oil

DIRECTIONS

1. Place the beans, tomato, bell pepper, corn, onion, jicama, jalapeno pepper, and feta cheese in a large salad bowl.
2. Mash the garlic and salt together with a mortar and pestle. Whisk together the mashed garlic, lime juice, mustard, and pepper in a small bowl. Add the oil in a slow, steady stream while whisking. Continue whisking until smooth. Drizzle the dressing over the salad and toss to coat. Chill overnight.

OPEN-FACED BROILED ROAST BEEF SANDWICH

Servings: 4 | Prep: 15m | Cooks: 5m | Total: 20m

NUTRITION FACTS

Calories: 397 | Carbohydrates: 23g | Fat: 19.2g | Protein: 34.4g | Cholesterol: 77mg

INGREDIENTS

- 2 hoagie buns, split
- 2 tomatoes, thinly sliced
- 2 tablespoons mayonnaise
- 1/2 red onion, thinly sliced
- 2 teaspoons prepared coarse-ground mustard
- 4 slices provolone cheese
- 1 pound deli sliced roast beef
- salt and pepper to taste

DIRECTIONS

1. Preheat oven on broiler setting.
2. Cut rolls in half, and toast in a bread toaster. Place on a baking sheet. Spread each half with mayonnaise and mustard. Layer with roast beef, tomato, red onion, Provolone, salt and pepper.
3. Broil 3 to 6 inches from heat source for 2 to 4 minutes (keep a constant eye on it) until cheese is bubbly and is beginning to brown.

HAM SALAD

Servings: 16 | Prep: 15m | Cooks: 0m | Total: 15m

NUTRITION FACTS

Calories: 278 | Carbohydrates: 7.3g | Fat: 24g | Protein: 9.9g | Cholesterol: 38mg

INGREDIENTS

- 2 cups mayonnaise
- 2 pounds smoked boneless ham, diced
- 1 cup sweet pickle relish
- 1 onion, diced
- 1/2 teaspoon freshly ground black pepper
- 1 small green bell pepper, diced
- 2 teaspoons salt
- 2 stalks celery, diced

DIRECTIONS

1. In a large bowl, stir together the mayonnaise, relish, pepper and salt until blended. Add the ham, onion, green pepper and celery and toss until coated. Store the salad, covered, in the refrigerator.

SUPER SEVEN SPINACH SALAD

Servings: 6 | Prep: 15m | Cooks: 0m | Total: 15m

NUTRITION FACTS

Calories: 138 | Carbohydrates: 12.5g | Fat: 8.3g | Protein: 3.8g | Cholesterol: 9mg

INGREDIENTS

- 1 (6 ounce) package baby spinach leaves
- 1/4 cup sweetened dried cranberries
- 1/3 cup cubed Cheddar cheese
- 1/3 cup blanched slivered almonds
- 1 Fuji apple - peeled, cored and diced
- 3 tablespoons poppy seed salad dressing
- 1/3 cup finely chopped red onion

DIRECTIONS

1. In a large salad bowl, combine the spinach, Cheddar cheese, apple, red onion, cranberries and slivered almonds. Toss with poppy seed dressing just before serving.

QUICK TUNA SALAD

Servings: 4 | Prep: 5m | Cooks: 0m | Total: 5m

NUTRITION FACTS

Calories: 142 | Carbohydrates: 4.4g | Fat: 5.9g | Protein: 16.7g | Cholesterol: 26mg

INGREDIENTS

- 1 (7 ounce) can solid white tuna packed in water, drained
- 1/4 cup creamy salad dressing (such as Miracle Whip™)
- 1 tablespoon sweet pickle relish, or to taste

DIRECTIONS

1. Mash tuna together with salad dressing and relish in a small bowl with a fork. Serve.

GRILLED CORN SALAD

Servings: 6 | Prep: 15m | Cooks: 10m | Total: 1h10m | Additional: 45m

NUTRITION FACTS

Calories: 103 | Carbohydrates: 19.7g | Fat: 2.8g | Protein: 3.4g | Cholesterol: 0mg

INGREDIENTS

- 6 ears freshly shucked corn
- 1/2 bunch fresh cilantro, chopped, or more to taste
- 1 green pepper, diced
- 2 teaspoons olive oil, or to taste
- 2 Roma (plum) tomatoes, diced
- salt and ground black pepper to taste
- 1/4 cup diced red onion

DIRECTIONS

1. Preheat an outdoor grill for medium heat; lightly oil the grate.
2. Cook the corn on the preheated grill, turning occasionally, until the corn is tender and specks of black appear, about 10 minutes; set aside until just cool enough to handle. Slice the kernels off of the cob and place into a bowl.

3. Combine the warm corn kernels with the green pepper, diced tomato, onion, cilantro, and olive oil. Season with salt and pepper; toss until evenly mixed. Set aside for at least 30 minutes to allow flavors to blend before serving.

SOUTHERN YANK PULLED PORK BBQ
Servings: 6 | Prep: 15m | Cooks:7h | Total: 7h15m

NUTRITION FACTS

Calories: 419 | Carbohydrates: 47.6g | Fat: 13.9g | Protein: 26.5g | Cholesterol: 89mg

INGREDIENTS

- 1 cup bottled barbecue sauce
- 1/4 cup light brown sugar
- 3/4 cup ketchup
- 1/4 cup Worcestershire sauce
- 1 1/4 cups chopped onion
- 1 1/2 teaspoons chili powder
- 1 cup chopped celery
- 1 tablespoon hot pepper sauce (such as Tabasco), or to taste
- 1 cup water
- salt and ground black pepper to taste
- 3 cloves garlic, chopped
- 1 (3 pound) pork shoulder roast
- 1/4 cup honey

DIRECTIONS

1. Mix together the barbecue sauce, ketchup, onion, celery, water, garlic, honey, brown sugar, Worcestershire sauce, chili powder, hot pepper sauce, salt, and black pepper in a slow cooker until thoroughly combined. Place the pork roast into the mixture, spoon sauce over the meat, and set the cooker to Low. Cook 7 to 8 hours; to serve, shred the meat with 2 forks, and serve with sauce.

OYAKODON (JAPANESE CHICKEN AND EGG RICE BOWL)
Servings: 4 | Prep: 15m | Cooks: 25m | Total: 40m

NUTRITION FACTS

Calories: 688 | Carbohydrates: 97.9g | Fat: 14.6g | Protein: 35.3g | Cholesterol: 208mg

INGREDIENTS

- 2 cups uncooked jasmine rice
- 1/4 cup soy sauce
- 4 cups water
- 3 tablespoons mirin (Japanese rice wine)
- 4 skinless, boneless chicken thighs, cut into small pieces
- 3 tablespoons brown sugar
- 1 onion, cut in half and sliced
- 4 eggs
- 2 cups dashi stock, made with dashi powder

DIRECTIONS

1. Rinse the rice in 3 to 4 changes of water until the rinse water is almost clear, and drain off the rinse water. Bring the rice and 4 cups of water to a boil in a saucepan over high heat. Reduce heat to medium-low, cover, and simmer until the rice is tender and the liquid has been absorbed, 20 to 25 minutes.
2. Place the chicken in a nonstick skillet with a lid, and cook and stir over medium heat until the chicken is no longer pink inside and beginning to brown, about 5 minutes. Stir in the onion, and cook and stir until the onion is soft, about 5 more minutes. Pour in the stock, and whisk in soy sauce, mirin, and brown sugar, stirring to dissolve the sugar. Bring the mixture to a boil, and let simmer until slightly reduced, about 10 minutes.
3. Whisk the eggs in a bowl until well-beaten, and pour over the chicken and stock. Cover the skillet, reduce heat, and allow to steam for about 5 minutes, until the egg is cooked. Remove from heat.
4. To serve, place 1 cup of cooked rice per bowl into 4 deep soup bowls, top each bowl with 1/4 of the chicken and egg mixture, and spoon about 1/2 cup of soup into each bowl.

MENDOCINO CHICKEN SALAD

Servings: 6 | Prep: 15m | Cooks: 1h | Total: 1h15m | Additional: 1h

NUTRITION FACTS

Calories: 365 | Carbohydrates: 12g | Fat: 32.2g | Protein: 9.5g | Cholesterol: 25mg

INGREDIENTS

- 1 (6 ounce) package smoked chicken breast, skin removed, cubed
- 1/4 cup fresh basil leaves, cut into thin strips
- 1 cup seedless grapes, halved
- 1 cup blanched slivered almonds
- 1/4 cup diced red onion

- 3/4 cup mayonnaise
- 3 stalks celery, diced

DIRECTIONS

1. In a large bowl, combine the smoked chicken, grapes, red onion, celery, basil, almonds, and mayonnaise. Mix well; chill and serve.

DOUBLE DECKER TACOS

Servings: 12 | Prep: 30m | Cooks: 15m | Total: 45m

NUTRITION FACTS

Calories: 458 | Carbohydrates: 37.3g | Fat: 26.3g | Protein: 18.9g | Cholesterol: 55mg

INGREDIENTS

- 1 pound ground beef
- salt and black pepper to taste
- 1 (1 ounce) packet taco seasoning mix, divided
- 12 (7 inch) flour tortillas
- 1 (16 ounce) can refried beans
- 2 cups shredded Cheddar cheese
- 2/3 cup water
- 1 cup shredded lettuce
- 12 prepared crisp taco shells
- 1 large tomato, chopped
- 2 avocados
- 1/4 red onion, chopped
- 1 tablespoon sour cream
- 1/2 cup sour cream
- 1 fresh lime, juiced

DIRECTIONS

1. Place the ground beef in a skillet over medium heat, and sprinkle about 3/4 of the packet of taco seasoning over the meat. Cook and stir the ground beef, breaking it up as it cooks, until the beef is browned and crumbly, 10 to 15 minutes. Drain the excess grease.
2. Mash the refried beans with the water in a small saucepan, and sprinkle with the rest of the seasoning packet. Heat the refried beans over low heat until simmering.
3. Preheat oven to 300 degrees F (150 degrees C). Place the crisp taco shells on a baking sheet, and warm them in the preheated oven for 3 to 5 minutes.

4. To make the guacamole, peel, seed, and mash the avocados in a bowl with 1 tablespoon of sour cream, the lime juice, and salt and pepper to taste, and set aside.
5. To build the tacos, spread each flour tortilla with about 2 tablespoons of heated refried beans. Wrap the tortilla gently around a crisp tortilla shell. Spread about 2 tablespoons of ground beef along the bottom of the crisp shell, and sprinkle about 2 tablespoons of shredded Cheddar cheese on top of the meat. Top the cheese with shredded lettuce, a sprinkle of chopped tomato and onion, and a dollop of sour cream and guacamole.

GREEK COUSCOUS

Servings: 3 | Prep: 20m | Cooks: 5m | Total: 45m

NUTRITION FACTS

Calories: 254 | Carbohydrates: 42.4g | Fat: 5.6g | Protein: 9g | Cholesterol: 6mg

INGREDIENTS

- 1/4 cup chicken broth
- 2 tablespoons crumbled feta cheese
- 1/2 cup water
- 1 cup canned garbanzo beans, rinsed and drained
- 1 teaspoon minced garlic
- 1 teaspoon dried oregano
- 1/2 cup pearl (Israeli) couscous
- 1/2 teaspoon ground black pepper
- 1/4 cup chopped sun-dried tomatoes
- 1 tablespoon white wine vinegar
- 1/4 cup sliced Kalamata olives
- 1 1/2 teaspoons lemon juice

DIRECTIONS

1. Pour the chicken broth and water into a saucepan, stir in the garlic, and bring to a boil. Stir in the couscous, cover the pan, and remove from heat. Allow the couscous to stand until all the water has been absorbed, about 5 minutes; fluff with a fork. Allow the couscous to cool to warm temperature.
2. In a large serving bowl, lightly toss the couscous, sun-dried tomatoes, olives, feta cheese, and garbanzo beans. Mix the oregano, black pepper, white wine vinegar, and lemon juice in a small bowl, and pour over the couscous mixture. Toss again to serve.

GREEK ZOODLE SALAD

Servings: 4 | Prep: 15m | Cooks: 10m | Total: 25m | Additional: 10m

NUTRITION FACTS

Calories: 147 | Carbohydrates: 9.1g | Fat: 11.1g | Protein: 5g | Cholesterol: 5mg

INGREDIENTS

- 2 zucchini
- 2 ounces crumbled reduced-fat feta cheese
- 1/4 English cucumber, chopped
- 2 tablespoons extra-virgin olive oil
- 10 cherry tomatoes, halved, or more to taste
- 2 tablespoons fresh lemon juice
- 10 pitted kalamata olives, halved, or more to taste
- 1 teaspoon dried oregano
- 1/4 cup thinly sliced red onion
- salt and ground black pepper to taste

DIRECTIONS

1. Cut zucchini into noodle-shaped strands using a spiralizing tool. Place "zoodles" in a large bowl and top with cucumber, tomatoes, olives, red onion, and feta cheese.
2. Whisk olive oil, lemon juice, oregano, salt, and pepper together in a bowl until dressing is smooth; pour over "zoodle" mixture and toss to coat. Marinate salad in refrigerator for 10 to 15 minutes.

MEATLOAF CUPCAKES

Servings: 6 | Prep: 20m | Cooks: 40m | Total: 1h

NUTRITION FACTS

Calories: 489 | Carbohydrates: 53.7g | Fat: 20.5g | Protein: 22.7g | Cholesterol: 100mg

INGREDIENTS

- 1 pound ground beef
- 2 cloves garlic, chopped
- 1 cup crushed saltine crackers
- 1 teaspoon ground black pepper
- 1/2 cup chopped onion
- 1 teaspoon seasoned salt
- 1/2 cup chopped green bell pepper
- 1/2 cup ketchup
- 1/3 cup milk
- 1/2 cup brown sugar

- 1 egg
- 4 cups mashed potatoes
- 1 tablespoon Worcestershire sauce
- 1 cup shredded Cheddar cheese

DIRECTIONS

1. Preheat oven to 350 degrees F (175 degrees C).
2. Mix ground beef, saltine crackers, onion, green bell pepper, milk, egg, Worcestershire sauce, garlic, black pepper, and seasoned salt together in a bowl.
3. Stir ketchup and brown sugar together in a bowl. Spoon ketchup mixture into the bottom of each muffin cup of a 6-cup muffin tin.
4. Fill muffin cups with beef mixture, leaving 1/2-inch space on the top.
5. Bake in the preheated oven until no longer pink in the center, about 30 minutes. An instant-read thermometer inserted into the center should read at least 160 degrees F (70 degrees C). Drain fat from muffin cups.
6. Top each 'cupcake' with mashed potatoes and Cheddar cheese.
7. Continue baking until cheese is melted, about 10 minutes.

Printed in Great Britain
by Amazon